THE JOHN CALVIN MCNAIR LECTURES
SPIRIT AND ITS FREEDOM

THE JOHN CALVIN McNAIR LECTURES

Francis H. Smith: *God Manifest in the Material Universe.*

Francis Landey Patton: *Authority and Religion.*

David Starr Jordan: *The Stability of Truth.*

Henry Van Dyke: *The Poetry of Nature.*

Arthur Twining Hadley: *Some Influences in Modern Philosophic Thought.*

Francis G. Peabody: *Christian Life in the Modern World.*

George Edgar Vincent: *The Social Vision.*

John Dewey: *Philosophy and Politics.*

Frederick J. E. Woodbridge: *The Purpose of History.*

Hugh Black: *The Great Questions of Life.*

Edwin Grant Conklin: *The Direction of Human Evolution.*

Paul Shorey: *Plato's Relation to the Religious Problem.*

Charles Allen Dinsmore: *Religious Certitude in an Age of Science.*

Roscoe Pound: *Law and Morals.*

William Louis Poteat: *Can a Man Be a Christian Today?*

Charles Reynolds Brown: *A Working Faith.*

Thornton Whaling: *Science and Religion Today.*

Harris E. Kirk: *Stars, Atoms, and God.*

Robert Andrews Millikan: *Time, Matter, and Values.*

George F. Thomas: *Spirit and Its Freedom.*

THE UNIVERSITY OF NORTH CAROLINA PRESS, CHAPEL HILL, N. C.; THE BAKER AND TAYLOR COMPANY, NEW YORK; OXFORD UNIVERSITY PRESS, LONDON; MARUZEN-KABUSHIKI-KAISHA, TOKYO; EDWARD EVANS & SONS, LTD., SHANGHAI; DEKKER EN NORDEMANN'S WETENSCHAPPELIJKE BOEK-HANDEL, AMSTERDAM.

SPIRIT AND ITS FREEDOM

By

GEORGE F. THOMAS

CHAPEL HILL
THE UNIVERSITY OF NORTH CAROLINA PRESS
1939

COPYRIGHT, 1939, BY
THE UNIVERSITY OF NORTH CAROLINA PRESS

TO THE MEMORY
OF
MY MOTHER

THE McNAIR LECTURES

THE John Calvin McNair Lectures were founded through a bequest made by Rev. John Calvin McNair, of the class of 1849. This bequest became available to the University in 1906. The extract from the will referring to the foundation is as follows:

"As soon as the interest accruing thereon shall by said Trustees be deemed sufficient they shall employ some able Scientific Gentleman to deliver before the students then in attendance at said University, a course of lectures, the object of which lectures shall be to show the mutual bearing of science and theology upon each other, and to prove the existence and attributes, as far as may be, of God from nature. The lectures, which must be performed by a member of some one of the Evangelic denominations of Christians, must be published within twelve months after delivery, either in pamphlet or book form."

PREFACE

A DISTINCTION is often made between the inner and the outer aspects of the life of a community. Both aspects must be taken into account in evaluating any community. Normally, the inner attitudes and ideas of its members are reflected clearly in the institutions of a community. When there is no close correspondence between the inner and the outer aspects of its life, however, the relationship between these aspects presents interesting and important problems. For instance, the inner life may be profoundly stirred and awakened without immediately changing the forms of institutional life. But tension or even revolution is sure to result. Or the animating spirit of a community may become decadent, while its institutions maintain themselves indefinitely in static fashion. Stagnation and disintegration then result. Is our social science or philosophy dealing with these relationships and the crucial problems set by them for our civilization? Whatever may be said of our social science, our contemporary philosophy is almost completely indifferent to them.

The only way to remedy this serious deficiency is to take up afresh the problems of the philosophy of spirit. The purpose of these lectures is to make a beginning in this direction. We wish to understand the nature of the spirit which moves in persons, gives dignity to their common life, and produces in them the fruits of culture. For this purpose we shall combine *historical* with *phenomenological* analysis. It is hoped that our historical analysis of Greek, Christian, and modern Idealistic conceptions of the spiritual life in the first chapter will enable us to define the crucial issues more precisely, as well as provide materials for our phenomenological analysis of spirit in the second chapter. An historical approach is the more necessary because the term "spirit," save when used in a loose sense, has almost disappeared from the vocabulary of educated men and women. One of the great needs of our time is for serious thinkers to rediscover the meaning of "spirit" in our long religious and philosophical tradition and to reinterpret it in such a way as to throw light upon the special problems of ethics, aesthetics, the social sciences, and the philosophy of religion.

The author has been especially influenced in his use of the phenomenological method in analyzing such concepts as "spirit," "love," and "freedom" by the examples of Max Scheler and Nicolai Hartmann who have applied it most fruitfully to the philosophy of spirit and to ethics. The method is simple in principle but difficult in application. Briefly, it seeks to concentrate upon an object of thought such as "spirit" in the various particular contexts in which it occurs, postpone all speculative questions concerning its ultimate metaphysical bearings, and gain an intuition of its essence as it is in itself. It holds that the essence of such an object can be understood, neither by inductive generalization from its appearances nor by deductive inference from other concepts, but only by direct insight. Thus it seeks to avoid both the error of empiricism, dogmatism of sense, and the error of rationalism, dogmatism of reason.

In the philosophy of spirit this method seems to the author to be especially fruitful, for the spirit reveals its essence and its mode of operation only to direct insight. But it is necessary to remember two things. First, the mind must have phenomena of the spiritual life before it if its insight into the nature of that life is to be significant. For this reason, the phenomenological method should be employed in close connection with the historical method referred to above. Second, the phenomenological method, even with the help of the historical method, cannot solve all of the problems of the philosophy of spirit. The author has said nothing about the Holy Spirit of Christian theology and very little about the Absolute Spirit of modern idealism. For the phenomenological method does not attempt to deal with theological or metaphysical problems such as the relation of the human spirit to the Divine Spirit. For that very reason, it would require to be supplemented by other methods. But the author has limited himself in what he has done to what he thought he could do.

Finally, the author wishes to express his gratitude for the help he has received from his former teacher, Professor W. H. Sheldon of Yale University; from his former colleagues at Dartmouth College, especially Professors W. K. Wright and A. Myrton Frye; from Professor David Roberts of Union Theological Seminary; and from his wife. He also wishes to thank those who were most responsible for making his visit to Chapel Hill as McNair Lecturer a happy one, especially Dean Francis Bradshaw and President and Mrs. Frank Graham.

GEORGE F. THOMAS

Chapel Hill, N. C.
March 8, 1939

CONTENTS

Preface · ix

I. Conceptions of Spirit 1

II. The Essence of Spirit 39

III. Freedom and the Spirit . . . 69

IV. Politics and the Spirit 113

SPIRIT AND ITS FREEDOM

CHAPTER I

CONCEPTIONS OF SPIRIT

THERE ARE THREE TERMS used by Plato which throw light upon his concept of spirit. The first of them is θυμός, which is often translated "spirit" or "the spirited element." Though Plato did not mean to signify by it the highest part or element of soul, he does say that normally it takes the side of the highest part in the struggle of the latter with appetite. It is the element which must be especially cultivated in and by the soldiers of the ideal republic, for when properly trained it is the basis of the virtue of courage characteristic of them. It must be remembered that the courage Plato required of his soldiers was not mere animal fury or recklessness, which might be regarded as an expression of instinct or impulse, but deliberate courage based upon right opinions about good and bad. Moreover, it is by θυμός that we are ashamed of ourselves when we yield to appetite against our better judgment, that we are aroused to indignation by an injustice done to us, that we are ambitious and desirous of honor, and the like. Thus, it might be said to mediate between appetite and reason. In the *Timaeus* this is expressed by locating it in the heart, between the head which is the seat of the intellect and the diaphragm below which the appetites reside. That it is not rational is shown by the fact that it can and often does ally itself with appetite rather than reason; thus, in the *Phaedrus* it is symbolized by the white, noble steed which is likely to follow after the black, vicious steed of appetite unless the rein of the charioteer reason is held firm. Θυμός, therefore, is not what we should call spirit; but it is capable of becoming an ally of spirit when correct education has brought it under control.

The second and most important term that throws light upon Plato's view of spirit is, of course, νοῦς, the rational part of the soul. Νοῦς in the human soul is that which contemplates the order of the cosmos. This means that it is defined not only as a subjective process in the soul, but also in terms of a relation of the soul to the objective structure of the world. The importance of this is seen when we realize that the structure or order of the world was conceived by Plato as universal Form. Thus, νοῦς is that element in the soul which apprehends or contemplates the universal. Now, the Forms or universals constitute true Being, as contrasted with the flux of the sensible world; and true Being is absolutely good. Therefore, νοῦς, in contemplating the Forms, becomes one with ultimate reality and absolute good. It raises the soul out of bondage to the physical appetites and narrow interests of the individual and enables him to participate in that which is most perfect and divine.

If there were any doubt that the activity of νοῦς is for Plato the life of the spirit, it would be dispelled by the way in which he links it with a third term, ἔρως. This term is usually translated "love"; in its higher meaning, it might be rendered "passion for truth and goodness." It seems to mean aspiration of the rational soul for the divine, an aspiration which is not capable of complete fulfillment because of the limitations of mortality but which may increasingly assimilate the soul to the divine and prepare it for an immortal life in the presence of the gods. As νοῦς means the contemplative possession of ultimate reality and goodness, ἔρως means the aspiration of the soul after that possession. In the *Symposium,* we are told that it is not divine but mediates between divinity and the soul; it is desire for an absolute beauty and goodness which the soul does not already possess. It is, Plato says, the offspring of Resource and Poverty, partaking of the qualities of both of its parents in that it both betrays the imperfections of the soul and reveals its passionate aspiration after perfection.[1] In short, ἔρως in its higher form contributes passion to the life of the spirit.

Thus νοῦς, with the aid of ἔρως, enables the soul to transcend the limits imposed by its body and its particularity and to rise into the realm of pure Being and universality. In doing so it helps the soul to recover its real nature which it has almost lost by its association with the body. For the essence of the soul lies in its kinship with the universal and divine. It is hard for us to realize this, caught as we are in the toils of bodily appetite and worldly ambition. But we can do so if we will purify ourselves by intellectual and moral discipline. "Its [the soul's] true nature," Plato says, "we must not examine in its present state, harmed as it is by communion with the body and other evils, but such as it is when pure.... We should look at its love of wisdom, consider what associations it reaches out to and longs for, how it is akin to the divine and the immortal, what it would become if it followed this longing entirely, and by that longing were lifted out of the sea wherein it now resides."[2] For the soul as we experience it in its embodied state is mixed, and its true nature obscured. Its lowest part, appetite, is the result of its association with a body, not an essen-

---

[1] It must be remembered, however, that ἔρως may take an "earthly" instead of a "heavenly" form; i.e., it may be degraded into a sensual and selfish craving for the body of the loved one.
[2] *Republic*, 611 b.

tial element of its nature. Its middle or "spirited" part is non-rational and requires to be disciplined by education before it can be regarded as an ally of reason. Only its highest part, reason, reveals its essential nature as akin to the divine and the universal. Only when the reason is inspired by love for the true and the good shining in their beauty, is the soul truly happy.

This does not mean that reason can be content with contemplation alone; indeed, Plato makes it abundantly clear that, however natural it may be for one who has come to know the eternal forms of Being to dread the shadows of time and Becoming, he must return to the cave and instruct his fellows in that which he has seen. This means that the soul is made not only to enjoy but to imitate the truth. Hence, the striking definition of love as the soul's desire for immortality which leads it to beget and bring forth truth in the beautiful. For as God imposed order and beauty upon matter and thus created the cosmos, so must the soul impose order upon itself and upon all that which surrounds it. As God has fashioned an orderly world, the lover of truth must fashion an orderly state; and not for his own sake alone, but for the sake of the harmony and happiness of all the citizens. If he does not gaze upon the Forms of true Being and fashion the laws and the education of the state after them, the harmony of the state will give way to discord, and the justice and temperance of the soul will be destroyed. Men will then live, not as rational souls with their gaze turned upwards towards the divine; but, in Plato's terrible words, "like cattle, with their eyes always looking down and their heads stooping to the earth, that is, to the dining table, they fatten and feed and breed, and in the excessive love of these delights, they kick and butt at one another with horns and hoofs which are made of iron; and they kill one another by reason of their insatiable lust."[3] Thus, the spiritual man, however little desire for political power he may have, cannot evade his responsibility for the order and justice of the city which nourished him. For Plato the spiritual life is at once austerely intellectual and intensely practical; in both respects, it is the very antithesis of sentimental otherworldliness.

The essence of Plato's conception of spirit may now be stated quite simply: the soul is spiritual so far as it is rational; and it is rational when it passionately desires to know and pattern its actions upon universal and eternal reality. He who is spiritual in this sense is happier than the sensualist or worldling, however much wealth or power the latter may possess to satisfy his insatiable desires; for the soul of the wise man is filled with the truest and highest pleasure derived from the truest and highest reality.

[3] *Republic*, 586 a.

CONCEPTIONS OF SPIRIT

In short, the spiritual life is rational, universal, and happy.

There are profound and noble insights in this doctrine; and it has become the basis of the dominant conception of spirit in European philosophy. There are, however, certain weaknesses in it which make it impossible for us to accept Plato's theory as adequate or final. It is worth while to remind ourselves of some of them if we would understand the significance of later conceptions. First, Plato's dualism of soul and body and of rational and irrational parts of the soul has generally been regarded as extreme. He does not, I think, lose sight of the unity of the soul. But he seems to have been greatly puzzled as to whether irrational elements of desire and feeling are parts of the soul as such, or are accidents due to its temporary sojourn in a body. In any case, desire and feeling, insofar as they depend upon and reflect the needs of the body, seem to be excluded from spiritual significance.

Second, Plato's restriction of the spiritual life to participation in universal truth and goodness negates the importance of individuality. The point we have just made about the body and the desires and feelings dependent upon it must be borne in mind here; for Plato tends to think of individuality in terms of materiality. The reason for this is that the body and its interests are particular and changeable, while the rational soul is turned towards the universal and immutable. As a consequence, the rational life of men is conceived in abstraction from their individual differences. The individual with his distinctive qualities is forgotten, all that counts is his relation to the universal. This depreciation of the significance of individuality for the higher life is one of the main causes of Plato's failure to appreciate the worth of personality. It leads to a view of the state which sacrifices persons and their freedom to the state and its order. It is also at the bottom of his criticism of art and poetry, for these are, he thinks, concerned with particular beautiful things, not with absolute and universal beauty. And it drives him to a view of love which is noble but inhumanly impersonal; for he sees the culmination of love in the intuition of absolute beauty rather than in devotion to persons.

Third, Plato's conception of truth and reality is abstract and static. The Forms or Ideas, though they may be suggested by sensible particulars, are conceived as eternal, immutable, and transcendent patterns. One result of this separation of the universal from the particular, the eternal from the temporal, is that reason is all but cut off from knowledge of the realm of time and change. It can have "opinions" of greater or less probability about things that "become," but it can gain true "knowledge" only of the eternal Forms that inhabit the realm of "Being." Plato's preference of mathematics and dialectic to biology is significant in this connection; and his neglect of the difference in method between abstract sciences like mathematics and concrete sciences like politics shows how impatient he was with the contingency and complexity of concrete existence. If knowledge is exclusively of the universal in abstraction from particulars, of the eternal in abstraction from existence in time, we must be content with mere opinions about concrete particulars and events, natural and human.

Finally, Plato's conception of creation as imitation of the eternal Forms in matter does scant justice to the uniqueness and spontaneity of creative activity. Creation is far more than the imposition of static Forms by a divine or human artist upon a given stuff. It is the production of novelty, not the copying of a finished perfection. It is no wonder, therefore, that Plato had a defective conception of will. Will cannot be identified with any of the three parts of the soul he distinguishes. He does appeal, again and again, to what we should call moral effort or resolution in urging men to devote themselves to the life of reason. But the dynamic for this effort does not seem to reside in will, but in love or passionate devotion to truth. He seems to have thought that knowledge is virtue, when it is accompanied by love of the good. But neither reason nor love nor a fusion of the two can take the place of the resolution and effort of will which are necessary to virtue.

Thus, Plato's false conception of creative action as the mere copying of static Forms may be the cause or the effect of his failure to recognize the unique nature of volition.

As is well known, Aristotle attempts to correct Plato's dualistic theory of the soul, his depreciation of the individual, his abstract and static conception of reality, and his blindness to the importance of will. To a considerable extent he succeeds, especially in his analysis of moral acts. Seeing the error in the Socratic maxim that knowledge is virtue, he points out that moral insight is dependent upon character, that character must be built up by the repetition of virtuous acts, and that the practical reasoning required for such acts differs from the theoretical reasoning of science. But though he seems to have many of the materials for a genuine concept of will as the faculty of action, he is unable wholly to escape from his Platonic premises. In his *De Anima*, he analyzes the nature of "desire" (ὄρεξις) as the efficient cause of motion in the body. But he does not seem to distinguish will from natural desire. In his *Nicomachean Ethics*, he treats "wish" (βούλησις) in such a way that it could have been easily distinguished from the particular desires. But, as Caird says, he does not regard it as "the essential impulse of rational nature" but only as "one of the elements of our being which is to be placed beside its other desires."⁴ Moreover, moral deliberation Aristotle defines "simply as a 'deliberative desire,' meaning a desire accompanied by deliberation as to the means of its satisfaction—a definition which leaves desire and reason as two separate elements which are connected only externally."⁵ Thus, Aristotle, despite the importance he attaches to practical action, does not really attain to a clear conception of will as distinguished from natural desire.

Similarly, he attempts to overcome Plato's dualism of soul and body by treating the soul as the form of its body. But he is unable to bring "active reason" (νοῦς ποιητικός) into organic relation with the body or with the lower psychical functions of sensation and desire. As a result, while the latter are conceived as closely related to the body, the "active reason" is treated as a sort of divine guest coming "from without" and sharing in the immortality of the gods. Thus, he is unable to escape from the Platonic dualism between the body and the lower elements of the soul, on the one hand, and the pure reason, on the other. Moreover, in his *Ethics* he sharpens the Platonic dualism between intellectual contemplation and practical action. The former, he says, is the most divine activity in human life since it enjoys the universal and necessary, while practical action is

⁴ Edward Caird, *The Evolution of Theology in the Greek Philosophers* (Glasgow, J. MacLehose & Sons, 1904), I, 316.
⁵ *Ibid.*, p. 317.

inferior since it concerns itself with the individual and contingent. By virtually restricting the spiritual life to intellectual contemplation in this manner, he seems to divorce it from political and moral action except as it depends upon such action for the basic conditions of its exercise. Moral and political action, on its side, loses contact with theoretical knowledge and becomes a practical matter of human happiness.

Thus, Aristotle does not escape from the worst defects of Plato's doctrine: its dualism and its emphasis upon contemplation at the expense of creation. Indeed, despite his greater interest in the concrete world of individuals, his conception of the life of the spirit is more detached, intellectualized, and abstract than that of Plato. He lacks both the passionate aspiration for beauty and goodness and the reforming zeal which have endeared his master to poets and statesmen alike. The drought of intellectualism had already begun to fall upon the Greek spirit. Henceforth, the living waters of the spirit were to run thin and dry; less and less could they refresh and stimulate the moral and political action and the artistic and poetic imagination of men. The Stoics, indeed, developed the conception of a universal, immanent reason ruling all nature and life with strict necessity; and out of this determinism arose a noble ethic of inner control and outer indifference. The Neoplatonists constructed a religious philosophy, according to which the enlightenment and emancipation of the soul could be attained only by union with the One. These schools of thought deepened the moral and religious consciousness, the one by stressing discipline and fortitude of will, the other by teaching the soul to unite itself with the Ground of all things. But they also tended to subordinate the creative effort of the spirit in the outer world. The Greek genius had not wholly spent itself; but it needed a new impulse and a new principle.

It was, of course, Christianity that provided the new point of view which was necessary for fruitful development.[6] For Christianity was strong precisely at the points where Greek philosophy was weak. This may be illustrated by a contrast between the dualism we have noted in Plato and the dualism to be found in the New Testament. In Plato, the primary dualism is that between the soul and the body, or between the rational and the irrational parts of the soul. Moral dualism, the radical opposition of good and evil, is also present in the

[6] It should be emphasized that in the account of Christianity which follows there are many omissions, most of which are due to the brevity of the treatment. Thus, nothing is said about the Christian doctrines of the Holy Spirit and of the initiative of God in the salvation of man through Christ. In addition, the treatment of the Kingdom of God and the effort of men in preparing for it emphasizes the human rather than the divine factor in the process. At all of these points, a metaphysic of spirit would be needed to supplement and modify the phenomenology of spirit, especially by making use of the evidence in Christian and other religious experience for the reality of a divine initiative and its transforming effects upon the spiritual life.

dialogues; but it rests upon this more fundamental dualism. Evil is due to animal appetite and wrong opinion, not to any defect of the will; indeed, as we have seen, Plato has no clear concept of the will. Hence, evil can be overcome only by the conquest of reason over appetite as the soul turns away from "opinion" of "Becoming" to "knowledge" of "Being." In the New Testament, on the other hand, moral dualism is primary rather than secondary. Evil is not mainly a matter of appetite or wrong opinion but of will. The conquest of evil, therefore, comes not from intellectual enlightenment but from repentance and faith followed by a transformation of the will.

A partial explanation of this striking difference is to be found in the fact that the Jewish tradition from which Christianity sprang did not associate evil with the body and its appetites as such. Though the body was compounded of the dust, it was part of the Creation which God looked upon and found good. The human being was treated concretely as an intimate union of body and soul, acting righteously or unrighteously as a whole self. That the soul considered by itself had no superior dignity is shown by the fact that in early Hebraism its joys were limited to its association with its body and its afterlife was a cheerless one; and when later Judaism arrived at the concept of a happy hereafter, it was not for souls as such but for righteous men, and it involved the resurrection of the body. Christianity has never been able to forget the eminently sane view of the body which it inherited from Judaism, however far it may have departed from it at times under the influence of pessimistic asceticism.

The body, then, is in itself good; men's evil deeds are the work of their evil wills. Again, we have seen that Plato's inadequate recognition of the will is closely related to his conception of creation as mere copying of a static reality. The case is quite different with the Hebrews. In the Old Testament account of Creation there is nothing corresponding to the eternal Forms which serve as the heavenly pattern for Plato's Creator when he fashions the world; rather, God creates by acts of will and thereby brings the Forms of things into being. Perhaps the most striking characteristic of the God of the early Old Testament is his creative will and power to execute his purposes. From the prophets onwards his power is connected with his holiness and his righteous judgments, and it tends more and more to become universal in scope. Moreover, the relation of his chosen people to him is defined in terms of moral action in carrying out his commands and purposes, rather than contemplation of his perfection or the perfection of his Creation. This is, of course, a matter of emphasis: the Psalms of adoration and of nature show clearly that contemplation of God's goodness and the sublimity of his Creation was not foreign to the Hebrew genius. But it is clear that righteousness of will and action as measured by God's commands is predominant. Thus, will rather than intellect is the center of the Hebraic conception of God and of man alike. It is obvious, on this view, that evil must reside in the will of man rather than in his appetites or his ignorance. The tragedy of man is that, destined to use the energy of his will in carrying out the purposes of God, he has rebelled against the commands of God. It was no accident that the Christian movement began with a Jewish prophet, John the Baptist, calling men to repentance, a radical turning of their wills from evil to good. Jesus' teaching stressed the necessity of definite decision, between God and Mammon, sincerity and hypocrisy, the narrow way and the broad way. One must make a radical break with the kingdom of this world and make ready for the new life of the Kingdom of God.

The higher estimate put upon the body and the central importance attributed to will and its action by Christianity are accompanied by a deepening of feeling. This is shown in many ways, not least by Jesus' insistence that inner purity is as important as outer conformity in matters of religious observance and moral rectitude. It is the spirit of sincerity and generosity that counts in fasting, alms-giving, and prayer, not the mere performance of the acts. It is freedom from anger and lust, not mere obedience

CONCEPTIONS OF SPIRIT 17

to the commands against murder and adultery, that is required. Motive is as significant as act; and the permanent disposition of the heart from which motive arises is important as the source of both act and motive. Hence the insistence in the Beatitudes upon mercy, purity, aspiration after righteousness and the like; hence also the position of love in religion and morals alike. There is nothing that throws more light upon the difference between Greek and Christian conceptions of the spiritual life than their treatment of love. Love (ἔρως) for Plato, as we have seen, means the dynamic and emotional aspect of the soul, the movement of desire toward the true as good and beautiful. Christian love (ἀγάπη), on the other hand, is not so much aspiration for an absent good as recognition of present good. It expresses itself in joyful affirmation of the being of him who is loved and in steadfast devotion to his welfare. It is not simply a movement of desire or feeling; it is a movement of will or, rather, of the whole self. For this reason it does not wax or wane as the natural feelings blow hot or cold; it is firm and loyal and enduring. For this reason, too, it can be directed towards enemies as well as friends and it can overlook barriers of race or class or creed. It does not content itself with sentiments but gives itself in helpful deeds. Thus Christian love is not a natural desire or feeling; it is essentially a spiritual act; indeed, it is the highest achievement of the spiritual life.

Moreover, the Platonic *Eros* in its highest form is the passion of the rational soul for the universal; but Christian love means the devotion of the whole self to persons. The essential difference between the Greek life of reason and the Christian life of the spirit lies here: the former exalts contemplation of the universal, the latter love of the individual. The contrast is, of course, not an absolute one. In Plato the particular reminds us of the universal, approximates it, participates in it, however much it falls short of it. We rise to the universal only by a dialectical process which starts with love of and opinions about the particular. And though love is impersonal in that its culmination is not in love of persons but in love of truth and beauty, we rejoice in the beauty and comradeship of loved friends on the way. Nevertheless, it remains true that for Plato the highest activity of man is contemplation of the universal. The heart of Christianity, on the other hand, is love of God and love of man as living and concrete individuals.

It is true that Christianity preaches the love of man, not for himself alone, but for his worth as a son of God. Man is what he is by virtue of his relation to God, the relation of an image or likeness to its original. That, in part, is what Christians mean when they say that the love of God is prior to the love of man; for God is the source of all good and pre-eminently of the goodness of man. Christian love is not identical with (though it may be the highest fulfillment of) the love of natural affection. As a settled disposition to devote oneself to the welfare of all persons, it rests upon belief in the potential worth of all persons as spiritual beings. In this respect, Christianity is far removed from modern humanitarianism in its estimate of man. Modern humanitarianism rests, in large part, upon the natural sympathy or fellow-feeling of the members of the human species for one another, and it is often associated with a romantic belief in the natural goodness of man. Christianity, save in its pessimistic forms, does not deny the value of natural sympathy nor the reality of man's potencies for good. But it is convinced that the highest love presupposes the intrinsic worth of man not as a member of an animal species but as a spiritual being.

The high estimate put upon the individual as a spiritual being does not, however, mean that Christianity has no interest in the universal. For the individual derives his significance, not only from the fact that he has been made in the image of God, but also from the fact that he is meant to participate in the universal creative work of God. It is in the concept of the Kingdom of God that the depth and vitality of the Christian view of the spiritual life shows itself most clearly. The Christian assertion of the dignity of man would be pointless if he had no destiny worthy of his dignity. But the concept of the Kingdom means that he does have such a destiny and that he is called actively to share in the working out of that destiny. He is a creature but his vocation is to create. And his work of creation is not merely for the sake of his own self-realization, the attainment of personal happiness or personal culture; his aim must be a universal one, the establishment of a community of love among all men.

This is, of course, the reason for the Christian emphasis upon the freedom of man. Freedom is of the essence of the Christian doctrine of man because it is his dignity as a son of God to ratify by his own free choice his divine calling to be a co-worker with God. Greek philosophy had not developed an adequate conception of freedom precisely because it had such an imperfect appreciation of will and its creativity. But the Christian conception of a Kingdom of God which requires the creative effort of man involves human freedom by its very nature. Indeed, it is because his freedom is given him to use in creative effort that his actual use of it is so tragic; for instead of choosing the high way he chooses the low. Sin is more heinous to the Christian than it was to the Greek because it is so much worse than a missing of the mark of human happiness because of impulse or ignorance; it is a perversion of the divine faculty of freedom given us for a sublime purpose.

Christianity, therefore, puts a high estimate upon the individual and his freedom, but not in abstraction from the universal purpose he is meant to serve. As the realm of eternal and immutable Being is the object of the Platonic *Eros,* the Kingdom of God is the object of Christian aspiration and effort. The individual must be willing to lose his life in devotion to this universal end, if he would save it. But though the end is universal, as in Plato, it is conceived in more dynamic and concrete terms. For the Kingdom of God is no mere static perfection, it is the end of a creative process in history, a universal community of persons bound together by mutual love. It is because of this conception of its universal end that the Christian life of the spirit seems so much less static and impersonal than the Greek. The Christian is called to love persons, not Forms; God, not Being; a community of men, not a system of universals.

The fruitfulness of the new ideas may be illustrated by a brief reference to medieval ethics. Christianity produced what Professor Gilson calls an "interiorization" of morality.[7] "The interior consent," he writes, "is already an act, as manifest to God as the exterior act is to man."[8] Indeed, Abelard goes so far in stressing the intention of the act that he actually regards an evil deed as adding nothing to the grav-

---

[7] Étienne Gilson, *The Spirit of Medieval Philosophy* (trans., A. H. C. Downes. London, Sheed & Ward, 1936), p. 344.
[8] *Ibid.*, p. 345.

ity of the sin.[9] In addition, conscience, the rational judgment of the agent upon the moral quality of his act, becomes all-important: "The will is now qualified, not by the object as it is in itself, but by the object as reason presents it; in itself indifferent, it becomes good or bad, according as reason proposed it as a good to be done or an evil to be avoided."[10] But the intention and conscience of the individual do not suffice by themselves to define moral obligation. Since our conscience may be erroneous, we are bound to enlighten it by reference to an ultimate end. The ultimate end for Aristotle is immanent in human life; it is human happiness through moral and intellectual virtue. But for Christians the ultimate end transcends human life; it is the service of God and His creative purpose. Hence, subjective intention and conscience must be measured by an objective and universal good beyond human life in its actuality.

Nor must morality alone be taken up into the spiritual life. Every human function and enterprise is to be devoted to the glory of God and the service of the community. Art, philosophy, politics and business are to be raised to a level suitable to the life of a spiritual community. Thus, the Catholic church in medieval Europe and the Puritan fathers of modern New England alike attempted to Christianize the whole of life. For one of the most distinctive things

[9] *Ibid.*, p. 349.   [10] *Ibid.*, p. 351.

about the Christian conception of the spiritual life, as we are now in a position to see, is its inclusiveness. For Plato the body and the appetites at the most might be tamed and forced to recognize the rule of reason over them. But Christians, with the exception of the ascetics, have dared to believe that the body and its desires can actually become instruments of spiritual life. Plato and Aristotle were convinced that his individuality must be left behind when a man contemplates the universal. But Christians have exalted the individual as of intrinsic worth as a son of God. Plato and Aristotle thought that only the noblest men could contemplate and imitate the universal. But Christians have urged all men, however simple and commonplace, to undertake the more difficult task of establishing a Kingdom of God among men and thus to join in the creative work of God himself. For the whole of life is to be transformed by the spirit, beginning with the individual will and its intention and extending to every institution and enterprise of humanity.

It is not my purpose to show how the Greek and Christian conceptions of spirit interacted with one another in medieval and early modern philosophy, nor to trace the idea of spirit in modern thought. All that is attempted in this chapter is a broad analysis of some of the main theories which have formed the dominant tradition concerning spirit in Western thought. The only modern theory which is comparable to the Greek and Christian theories in importance is that of German Idealism, especially as it is developed by Hegel into a comprehensive philosophy of spirit.

Spirit, as Hegel conceives it, is a subjective principle which determines itself. In nature, objects and events are contingent, each being determined by others rather than by itself. Nature, in other words, is the sphere of externality and reciprocal determination. Spirit, on the contrary, determines itself and is in that sense free. But its subjectivity and self-determination are not to be thought of abstractly, as in Descartes' theory of *res cogitans*. Spirit is not pure subjective activity independent of its world. As Reyburn puts it, "If we abstract from the objective content of the mind, from . . . its world of environment, we leave standing nothing but a void form,"[11] the form of mental activity without content. Hence, though spirit determines itself from within, it does so in relation to that which is without. A subjective principle that acted only within itself, like the Prime Mover of Aristotle, would not be spirit. Spirit must go forth from its subjectivity, confront itself with an objective world, and thus realize itself in and through that which is other than itself.

[11] H. A. Reyburn, *The Ethical Theory of Hegel* (Oxford, Clarendon Press, 1921), p. 80.

This means that though nature is other than spirit, it is also one with it. When the facts of nature are understood, they lose their externality. On the one hand, mind rises in nature and draws its content from the outer world; on the other hand, "the natural is transformed and idealized when it becomes spiritual; it achieves a unity and constitutes a system which is mind and not nature."[12] Thus, spirit in the process of objectifying itself in nature, internalizes or spiritualizes nature. Nature is other than and opposed to spirit, but spirit includes and subordinates nature as a moment of its own being.

The reason for this self-determination of spirit by self-objectification is that spirit fulfills itself only in self-consciousness. Now self-consciousness arises when the subject and its object become one, the subject finding itself in the object which at first confronted it as an alien thing. The theoretical reason, on its side, discovers that the object which appeared external and contingent is in reality part of a system which is intelligible through and through. Thus the more reason understands the structure of the external world the more it finds itself in it. The practical reason, on its side, finds that the social institutions and moral duties which seemed to restrict the freedom of the self, in reality render its freedom more effective. As theoretical reason internalizes the external, practical reason externalizes ideas which

[12] *Ibid.*, p. 84.

were internal. When the objective and the subjective are discovered in this way to be one, the spirit finds nothing but itself wherever it turns. Thus, that self-consciousness is realized which Hegel speaks of as the Absolute Idea, at once the highest category of thought and the ultimate reality.

This process by which spirit is revealed to itself is a dialectical one. Self-consciousness arises only through the recognition and the overcoming of oppositions. The spirit must find itself in that which is other than itself, because its identity is concrete and includes differences. It is infinite in the sense that it transcends all limits, in the very act of recognizing them as limits making the necessity which confronts it the instrument of its freedom. The philosophy of spirit is the analysis of the major stages traversed by spirit as it overcomes the oppositions or contradictions which confront it and thus attains to self-consciousness. Nature is the first and lowest stage of the process because, as we have seen, nature is the sphere of externality most obviously opposed to the internality of spirit. But spirit returns to itself from the otherness of nature, rising by stages to full self-consciousness.

Subjective spirit is the most abstract form of spirit as spirit. It is spirit on the side of its abstract form, considered not as realizing itself objectively but merely as a feeling, thinking, and willing self. As Reyburn puts it, it is "the immediate mode of

CONCEPTIONS OF SPIRIT

mind, its self-contained being, not yet articulated into a world other than itself."[13] Its interest for us lies in the fact that for Hegel it includes processes such as feeling and appetite which would usually not be regarded as belonging to spirit at all. As a monistic idealist, Hegel has set himself the task of interpreting all reality as the manifestation of a spiritual principle. In order to do so, we may suggest, he is forced to extend the meaning of spirit to the point of including everything subjective. When it is thus extended, it threatens to become meaningless.

Objective spirit is spirit which has gone out of itself and embodied itself in a world of social institutions and duties. Here, too, Hegel's determination to find spirit everywhere, in our opinion, leads him into excesses. Among these excesses is his glorification of the state as the "Divine Idea on earth." The cardinal error here is not the assertion of a spiritual factor at work in the state, but the neglect of other factors which accompany and limit it, for example, the economic interests of groups and the political ambitions of leaders. Hegel is, of course, aware of the existence of these non-spiritual factors. But he unduly subordinates the economic foundations of the state to its cultural fruits; and he glosses over the egoism and ruthlessness of a Caesar as the "cunning" of the World-Spirit in using even selfish passions to serve its spiritual ends. Thus the peculiar complex-

[13] *Ibid.*, p. 91.

ity of organized society, as a product of biological, economic, and political interests, no less than spiritual aspirations, is neglected.

Absolute spirit, Hegel says, is the synthesis of Subjective and Objective spirit. In it the spirit has returned to itself out of its other and attained to self-consciousness. In art, religion, and philosophy the finite spirit becomes aware of its unity with the infinite and universal spirit immanent in it. What is most striking about Hegel's conception of these three phases of Absolute spirit is that they are all essentially forms of knowledge. Art is the embodiment in sensuous form of the Idea. Religion is the imaginative conception of the Idea and its unity with humanity. Philosophy is the apprehension of the Idea in conceptual form. The object of all three is the same, it is only the forms in which it is expressed that differ. As knowledge by means of concepts is superior to knowledge by means of sense and imagination, philosophy is the highest of the three in its form. Hence, art and religion are in a sense naïve and inferior forms of philosophy. More than once Hegel recognizes the uniqueness and autonomy of art and religion, and the fact that he devotes long treatises to them bears witness to their importance in his mind. But this does not change the fact that for him art and religion are lower stages of the self-revelation of the Absolute Idea, while philosophy—

his own, at any rate—represents the highest self-consciousness.

Artists and religious people have naturally rejected this doctrine. Both art and religion provide intuitions of reality, especially with respect to its value and purpose, which are distinctive and cannot be replaced by the conceptual interpretation of philosophy. It is true that Hegel's recognition of the theoretical value of artistic and religious imagination, the content of which he regards as identical with that of philosophy, assigns places of dignity to them. Few rationalists have gone as far as he in this direction. But his assimilation of them to philosophy threatens their autonomy nevertheless. For the distinctive contribution of art and religion to the spiritual life lies, not simply in the theoretical insights they contain, but in the affirmation of intrinsic value by art and the faith of religion in the cosmic importance of the spirit and its values. They are well-defined elements in the spiritual life and it is meaningless to speak of philosophy as a synthesis of them. The truth is, it is impossible to acquit Hegel of the charge of intellectualism at this point, despite the efforts of his admirers to do so. As Croce has said, art and religion are not to be dialectically transcended in philosophy; they are not "opposites" inviting a synthesis of their conflicting claims but "distincts" enjoying an autonomous existence of their own.[14]

We have suggested certain flaws in Hegel's conceptions of the Subjective, Objective, and Absolute spirit. What are we to say of his conception of spirit *in general*? Is spirit essentially a process of self-fulfillment through self-objectification? Does its self-fulfillment have as its end self-consciousness? I believe that the first of these questions must be answered in the affirmative, the second in the negative. Hegel's most profound insight is that spirit is not static substance but dynamic activity. Though he was influenced by Aristotle's dynamic conception of actuality, his thinking at this point is really more Christian than Greek. As we have pointed out, the Greek philosophers tend to conceive of the divine mind as enjoying static perfection and of the human mind as imitating that perfection in contemplation. Christians, on the other hand, have thought of God as dynamic will and of His sons as actively preparing themselves for His Kingdom. For Christians, God is not self-sufficient but providential in His relation to the Creation; in Hegel's terms, He fulfills Himself in objectifying Himself in nature and human spirit. And as God is Himself only as He pours forth His grace upon His creatures, so men attain their spiritual dignity only as they love and

[14] Benedetto Croce, *What is Living and What is Dead of the Philosophy of Hegel* (trans., Douglas Ainslie. London, Macmillan, 1915), Chap. IV.

serve their fellows. Thus, the subject must be confronted by and lose itself in an object before it can rise to the level of spirit. Spirit rests upon objectivity.

But this profound insight is largely obscured by Hegel's idealistic insistence that the objectivity of spirit exists for the sake of a higher subjectivity, that spirit confronts itself with its other only to find itself in its other and return triumphantly into itself. Why should it be assumed that the divine spirit has gone forth from itself into nature and humanity to realize its own nature as self-consciousness? Has Hegel emancipated himself at this point from Aristotle's theory that the highest blessedness is that of the divine contemplation of itself? It is true that Aristotle's God is transcendent and his self-consciousness in no sense includes the world, whereas Hegel's God is immanent in the world and its infinite self-consciousness includes all its finite manifestations. But though the Absolute is in all of its appearances, it is in none of them; all are necessary as moments of its life, but each is overcome and absorbed into itself. In the end, therefore, the objectivity of the Absolute is but a veiled subjectivity.

Of course, this is logically required by Hegel's monism. If intelligibility requires complete organic unity, all oppositions must be overcome in this unity. Reason must proceed dialectically, opposing thesis to antithesis and overcoming their contradiction in a higher synthesis which is the unity of both. In this way, reason must reach at the end of the dialectical process a synthesis which contains within itself all of the earlier moments and reconciles their contradictions within itself. This unity, it is true, is no abstract identity but a concrete system. But the important thing is that the unity of the system is the presupposition of its diversity, so that all contradictions, however ultimate they may seem to be, must be reconciled in it.[15] Among these contradictions (or oppositions), that between Subject and Object is one of the most stubborn. Even if Hegel's identification of subject and object in self-consciousness constituted an adequate solution of the problem of knowledge, it would not provide a satisfactory basis for the philosophy of spirit. In the moral and religious consciousness, especially, the human spirit is confronted by a moral ideal and a divine Reality which are other than itself. To deny the otherness of God in relation to man and the world is to fall into pantheism; to deny the opposition of the moral ideal to much of human life is to deny the reality of moral evil.

But the opposition between subject and object is not the only real opposition which is "overcome" in Hegel's monism. His identification of the Individual with the Universal is equally dubious. In ethics it leads to a determination of the conscience of the in-

[15] On this point, see Edward Caird's *Hegel* (Edinburgh, W. Blackwood & Sons, 1899), Chap. VII.

dividual by society, in politics to a narrow limitation of his freedom by the state, in art and religion to a subordination of the particular object and historical fact to their universal significance.[16] But spirit as we know it is individual, a person is not a mere pulsation in the life of the World-Spirit nor a mere cell in a social organism, and the true relation of spiritual persons to the universal is not one of ontological identity but one of free devotion.

Finally, and above all, we must reject Hegel's monistic identification of the Ideal with the Real. Platonic idealism and Christian theism are at one in refusing to make such an identification. It leads to an unrealistic optimism in religion, to a deduction of norms from facts in ethics, and to a sanctification of the *status quo* in politics. It is no adequate defense of Hegel to say that he identifies the Ideal, not with *existence* as such, but with its essential meaning or *reality*. To argue in this way is merely to beg the question at issue, the question whether all existence *can* be shown to be ideal. A less optimistic but more sane philosophy of spirit will not reduce the Ideal to the level of the Real or sanctify the Real as Ideal, but will recognize that creative spiritual activity is directed to the slow and imperfect realization of the Ideal in the Real. Thus, it will agree with Hegel that spirit involves a process

[16] A good example of this in religion is Hegel's tendency to minimize the importance of the historical Jesus by making him a mere illustration of the union of the divine with all humanity.

of self-fulfillment through self-objectification in its other. But it will deny the inference that in its world it meets only with that which is ideal. With Hegel, it will find in nature and in art a revelation of the spirit; in social morality a partial victory of good over evil; in religion a prophetic anticipation of the more complete redemption of the real by the ideal. But neither in nature nor in society nor in the highest achievements of culture will it ever claim to find more than a partial and imperfect manifestation of the spirit.

In summary, our criticism of Greek, Christian, and Hegelian theories of spirit has revealed the crucial importance of certain issues which must be kept in mind as we attempt in the next chapter to analyze spirit for ourselves. The first of these issues concerns the place of intellect and will in the spiritual life. The Greek theory puts intellectual contemplation of truth definitely into the foreground. Will, insofar as it is distinguished from natural desire, is conceived as determined by knowledge. Evil is due, not to badness of will, but to error or impulse. The Christian theory, on the other hand, conceives more clearly the nature of the will as a principle which initiates acts reflecting the good or evil character of the person as a whole. It is not on that account a "voluntaristic" theory. For though the will is given greater prominence, love which gives direction to the will is more fundamental still. But there is a deep interest in will, motive, and action ("fruits"), as expressing the good or evil of the whole person. Evil is therefore traced to the will, not as one faculty of the self, but as the whole self in action. On the whole, the Hegelian view is Greek rather than Christian on this issue, since spirit is thought and will is simply thought in action.

The second issue has to do with the place of individuality. Broadly speaking, the Greek theory depreciated individual differences and exalted correspondingly the universal nature and ends shared by all rational and civilized men, that is, by all Greeks. The highest good of the individual as a social being was participation in the common life of his city-state. His highest good as a spiritual being lay in contemplation of universal truth, the reason in him apprehending the rational order of the cosmos around him. The Christian theory, on the other hand, gives central importance to the individual and his salvation. It stresses his worth as a unique being and regards him as fundamentally equal with all others whatever his class or race. Hegel attempts a synthesis by identifying the individual with the universal. In effect, however, the autonomy and significance of the individual are subordinated by him to the social organism and to the universal spirit of which he is only a part.

It will have been noticed that the Greek and

Hegelian theories, which give priority to intellect, subordinate the individual to the universal, while the Christian theory, which gives a certain prominence to the will, raises the individual to a position of greater importance. There is a similar correlation with regard to the third issue, which concerns the nature of the universal end. The universal contemplated by intellect is abstract, impersonal truth; the universal served by will is concrete, personal good. We have pointed out that Platonic love is directed towards truth and beauty, Christian love towards persons. The difference is not that the Christian has no interest in a universal end, but that he devotes himself to a universal end that is concrete. The Kingdom of God is nothing apart from the persons who constitute its members, it is simply the rule of God in the hearts and lives of all persons. Christian love is not love of humanity in the abstract, but love of one's neighbor. Hegel's position on this issue is ambiguous. The universal spirit is concrete; it is realized in nature and humanity. But it is not conceived in personal terms. Here, then, Hegel represents a compromise between Christian and Greek theories.

The fourth issue has to do with the relation of the spirit to the other elements of personality. The Greek theory identified the life of the spirit with the life of reason and set it apart from body and its desires. The wise man must be above, if not immune to, the "disturbances" of appetite and passion which originate in the body. The relation of soul to body might be treated dualistically by Plato or more naturalistically by Aristotle, but in neither case is the body really a partner with reason in the spiritual life. The Christian theory, on the other hand, does not confine spirit to the life of reason alone, but seeks to make the whole personality spiritual. Not only the will, but the self as a whole, its thoughts, desires, and feelings, are to be transformed. The body also must be purified of its characteristic vices of gluttony, lust, and the like, for it is the temple of God. At this point, the Hegelian theory is more Christian than Greek, in the sense that spirit is all-inclusive. This is due to the fact that a monistic idealism requires the presence of spirit everywhere, even in nature. The non-rational elements of the self, however, share in the spiritual life, not in their own non-rational character, but as less developed manifestations of reason.

The fifth and last issue is one which is only suggested by the theories we have examined, but which is put into high relief by their contrast with more naturalistic and realistic theories of contemporary thought. Greek, Christian, and Hegelian theories are at one in giving pre-eminence to spirit and its values in the world. Christian theism has faith in God's providential grace, Platonic idealism (with less assurance), in the moral efforts of wise men to bring life into harmony with the spirit and its ideal. Hegel asserts with sublime optimism that the real is already rational through and through. But contemporary naturalists like Santayana deny efficient causality to spirit and final causality to its values. Realists like Scheler and Hartmann are struck by its weakness in the midst of the natural forces that seem so strong in the world. Does the spirit possess power? If so, is its power really its own or does it represent a mere "sublimation" or overflow of biological energy? Is its power sufficient to master the forces that are alien to it? Or is it at best an aspiration without capacity to realize itself in human life? These crucial questions cannot be solved by the phenomenological method alone without recourse to metaphysical theory or religious faith. But to them, as to the other questions we have raised, we must suggest at least a partial and provisional answer.

CHAPTER II

THE ESSENCE OF SPIRIT

WE SHALL APPROACH our own analysis of spirit by referring briefly to the theory of Max Scheler, a distinguished representative of the "phenomenological" school in recent philosophy.[1] Spirit *(Geist)* is the distinctive characteristic of man, Scheler holds, and as such is to be contrasted with life *(Leben)* which man shares with all animals. Whereas life reacts only to the surrounding objects upon which the fulfillment of impulse depends, spirit is able to free itself from its physical environment by elevating physical objects to the status of objects of thought. In this way it expands the scope of attention and conceives a wider world *(Welt)* than its immediate environment *(Umwelt)*. The importance of this process is that it enables us to achieve objectivity in relation to our world. If we master the life-impulses which bind us to things as they concern our animal

[1] *Die Stellung des Menschen im Kosmos* (Darmstadt, O. Reiche, 1928).

interests, we can become "open" to the world, receptive to its intrinsic and essential character. Hence, discipline of impulse is the condition of spiritual activity, freeing us from a purely biological relation to our environment and making vital energies available for the spiritual life.

Scheler also distinguishes spirit from intelligence in the service of life (*praktische Intelligenz*). Intelligence is a function of soul (*Seele*), that is, the series of psychical events which accompany the series of bodily changes. It arises out of the capacity of the soul to remember its past states, associate them in certain ways, and bring them into relation with the needs of the present. The practical intelligence is thus qualitatively different from spirit. For the primary function of practical intelligence is to bring the body into effective relation with the physical objects which fulfill its impulses.

Spirit, on the other hand, opens itself to the objective reality of the world. It does so primarily by intuiting the essences (*Wesen*) of things independently of the contingent and accidental aspects of their appearance here and now. For example, a pain felt in my arm at this moment concerns life only as a particular evil to be escaped; but it may suggest to spirit the universality of evil in the world.[2] In other words, a spiritual being possesses the capacity to separate essence from existence, universal

[2] *Ibid.*, p. 60.

THE ESSENCE OF SPIRIT

meaning from particular fact.³ We must not, of course, think of the spirit (nor even of the person to whom it belongs) as a substance. Rather, the person is a center of spiritual acts *(Aktzentrum)* with a certain structure. These acts include, not only intuitions of essence, but also acts of pure love directed towards objective values and acts of pure will directed towards the realization of these values. We may say, therefore, that spirit is the activity of a person in devoting his vital energies to the apprehension of essences by intuition, the appreciation of objective values by love, and the realization of goods by will.

It will be seen at once that Scheler's phenomenology of spirit attempts to synthesize several elements of the Greek and the Christian traditions. It is Platonic in its sharp distinction between life and spirit. It is Platonic also in its stress upon the intellectual intuition of essences and the love of objective values. But it is Christian in its view of individual persons as centers of spiritual acts and in the importance it attributes to will. Above all, it is Christian in its conception of reality as dynamic rather than static. The meaning of the world for Scheler lies in the struggle of Cosmic Spirit to impose its control upon the blind drive of Impulse *(Trieb)*. This it can do only by leading and directing Im-

³ *Ibid.*, p. 62.

pulse, holding up before it as ideals the essences and values which Spirit intuits and loves.

Spirit can master life only to the extent that it can "persuade" it, "sublimate" its energies; for spirit has no energy of its own. In this last respect, Scheler's conception seems to be more influenced by the voluntarism of Schopenhauer, Freud, and others than by Christian theism. To the Christian, human spirit by itself is a weak reed in the face of the powers of this world, but it is fortified by the divine Being upon whom it depends. But Scheler, impressed with the lack of power in human spirit completely to master impulse, interprets the World-Ground as containing within itself a blind drive of Impulse as well as the Spirit that seeks to master it. As a result of this dualistic conception, spirit is regarded as higher than impulse in excellence but weaker in power. Nevertheless, though it is without energy of its own, it is able to discipline and direct impulse to a certain extent by holding up ideals before it and using the energies of impulse for its own ends.

We may begin our own analysis of the nature of spirit by stressing Scheler's point that spirit denotes a *mental activity* which occurs at a high level of human experience. We may think of this activity as habitual and characteristic, or we may think of it as rare and fleeting, in a given person. In any case, it is primarily an activity, not a static quality. But it carries with it a definite quality, which can be intuited. It is this quality to which we refer when we speak of spiritual activity as taking place at a "high level" of experience. Now, to say that it is an activity is to say that it is not a thing in the ordinary sense of that word. It is all too easy to fall into the habit of substantializing it because we use the term "spirit" or "the spirit" as if it were an entity residing in the body or the soul or both. One way to avoid this danger is to use the adjective "spiritual" rather than the noun "spirit." But this too is misleading in that it refers to the quality but not the activity to which the quality belongs. The term "spiritual activity" is more accurate, since it designates both the activity and its qualitative character.

We must, then, conceive of the spirit, not as a thing nor as a quality of a thing, but as the spiritual activity of a person. Now, spirit seems to be both one kind of activity and a principle that can affect all the activities of the self. When we speak of spirit or spiritual activity, therefore, we must be on our guard not to separate it too sharply from the other aspects of the self's activity, as if the self were divided into a number of parts as external to one another as the organs of its body. We have seen that one of the major weaknesses in Plato's theory of spirit was his elevation of reason so high above the irrational elements of the soul that the latter were cut off from all spiritual significance. Christianity, at least in its original form, does not make this mistake, for it considers a person as a concrete whole, all of whose functions can be given a spiritual meaning. But a distinctively spiritual activity must exist at its center before the whole of the personality can be spiritualized. The Hegelian view that spirit is present even in the lowest forms of the soul's experience, for example, in sensation, is true in the sense that these forms are capable of being taken up into and enriching the spiritual life. But it tends to blur the distinction between what is and what is not distinctively spiritual in experience, destroying the meaning of the term by making it too inclusive. Rather, spirit is one kind of mental activity distinguishable from others, but it is also capable of permeating and transforming the whole of experience.

Perhaps we may best approach the problem of defining the distinctive character of this spiritual activity by pointing out what it is not. First, it is to be distinguished from *life*. Under the influence of Vitalism, we are accustomed to using the term life in an honorific sense and we easily forget that life for the biologist simply designates the sum of organic functions such as growth, nourishment, and reproduction. These vital functions obviously cannot be separated from the elementary psychical functions of sensation, impulse, and feeling with which they are associated, for these are also concerned in

THE ESSENCE OF SPIRIT

the first instance with the maintenance and health of life. Now, spirit is related to these psycho-physiological functions in that it depends upon them for its existence and draws from them much of the stimulus for and content of its own activity. In many and subtle ways the life of the spirit is influenced by the fortunes of the body and the flow of its energies. Nevertheless, spiritual activity is directed towards distinctive objects and ends of its own quite different from those of the body. It is for this reason that the discipline of impulse is necessary; and sometimes it may be carried so far that life is denied. Indeed, renunciation of life in a certain measure is absolutely necessary to the spirit's activity in its more intense forms. The current habit of confusing spirit with vitality is possible only because we have come to prize physical health and external and lively activity more than inner excellence. There is a real danger of spirit's becoming identified, as in Nazi ideology, with hard and heroic living for the sake of power, or of its being more subtly confused, as by Bergson, with an upward but irrational thrust of life.

Again, we must not identify spirit with the whole *self,* or even with the whole *mind.* It is not the self, for self includes the whole personality, not simply its spiritual activity. Its relation to mind is more difficult. As practical intelligence, mind is primarily an instrument in the service of life, as Bergson, Scheler, and others have pointed out. But "mind" may be used more broadly to mean all of the acts and contents of experience, conscious and perhaps subconscious. "Mind" in this sense, includes both the elementary psychical processes which accompany and serve biological functions and also those acts and contents of thinking, willing, remembering, imagining, and the like which have little or no relation to vital ends. Thus, mind both serves life and maintains an independent activity of its own through the free play and wide range of its ideas. For this reason spirit can neither be identified with mind in the whole range of its experience nor can it be divorced from mind. Perhaps we may say, provisionally, that spirit is mind insofar as mind is directed towards ultimate reality and absolute value.

In this way, we can treat spirit as mental and at the same time distinguish it from other forms of mental activity. A clever and successful rogue has mind, but he is obviously not a spiritual man. What does he lack? The popular reply would be that he lacks moral responsibility and *goodness*. But though moral responsibility and goodness may be a part of, it is not identical with, the spiritual life. A fundamental weakness in Kant's doctrine of the higher life of man is that he is able to see very little difference between moral goodness (based upon respect for the moral law) and the spiritual life. Wherein does moralism of this sort fall short of the spiritual life? Perhaps the simplest answer is that the sense of responsibility of the Kantian moralist is a matter of the reason and will rather than the whole mind; hence, he acts from duty, not from devotion. His goodness is not inspired and elevated by love. He does what he should, but he does not forget himself in his cause. It must be remembered, too, that morality is not always "rational" in Kant's sense; it may be "conventional" or it may be "prophetic." But "conventional" morality requires mere conformity to custom and is a matter of social exigency rather than spiritual aspiration. "Prophetic" morality, on the other hand, inspired as it is by an intuition of the unity of all humanity as sons of God, is spiritual. Spirit, then, is not to be identified with moral goodness as such, though "prophetic" morality is an important aspect of spiritual life. So spirit is not life, it is not goodness as such. It is a distinctive activity of mind, able to transform life and to raise goodness to its own level.

Let us try to indicate some of its major aspects, remembering that what analysis must separate, intuition reveals as a unity. First, then, spirit is *personal*. On this point we must break decisively with the Greek and align ourselves with the Christian theory. We know no spiritual activity which does not originate in individual persons. By itself, this does not define the nature of spirit; indeed, taken by itself it reveals little of the spirit's distinctive character. But it is fundamental to the aspects of spirit which are distinctive, and if it is denied, spirit is easily confused with impersonal vital or physical processes. To overlook the fact that spiritual activity issues from an individual person is to render freedom meaningless and to degrade will into an expression of physical force or vital impulse. This is the danger of a voluntarism like Schopenhauer's or Nietzsche's. There is a somewhat similar danger in the idealism of Hegel. There is a famous passage in Hegel's *Philosophy of History* in which he speaks of "the cunning of reason that it sets the passion [of individuals] to work for itself, while that which develops its existence through such impulsion pays the penalty and suffers loss." "The particular," he says, "is for the most part of too trifling value as compared with the general: individuals are sacrificed and abandoned."[4]

As against this conception of the individual, we must affirm the Kantian view that a person is an end in himself. But a person possesses spiritual worth only insofar as he freely serves super-personal ends; and the quality of his individuality is defined, not by the separate existence of his body, but by the unique way in which he devotes himself to universal truth and value. Hence, individuality need not be lost in devotion to the universal, as Plato implied; indeed it can find itself only in relation to the uni-

[4] G. W. F. Hegel, *Lectures on the Philosophy of History* (trans., J. Sibree. London, H. G. Bohn, 1861), p. 34.

versal. Nothing illustrates this better than the way in which a great artist suggests universal meanings in a way characteristic of himself as an individual. "The Last Supper" of Leonardo and the "Creation of Man" by Michelangelo are universal themes but they are treated in thoroughly individual ways. In the same way, Aquinas and Dante expressed the same world-view each in his own medium and with his own characteristic emphasis.

In the second place, then, the spiritual activity of an individual is that which is directed towards *universal* truth and value. It is by his identification of himself with the universal that a person enters the spiritual life. The reason for this lies in that capacity for "self-transcendence" which is the glory of mind. The most profound thing in Plato's theory of love is his statement that it indicates at once a defect of being on the part of the soul and an aspiration to overcome that defect by seeking to possess the perfection it lacks. Similarly the Scholastics hold that, though the human soul is finite, it has an aspiration that can be filled with nothing short of the infinite. Spirit involves a kind of union of the individual with the universal.

But everything depends upon the way in which the universal and the union of the individual with it is conceived. We have seen that in Plato's theory the universal is impersonal and abstract, whereas in the Christian theory it is personal and concrete. The

Platonist devotes himself to Being, to absolute truth, beauty, and goodness. The Christian, on the other hand, devotes himself to the Kingdom of God conceived as an ideal community which includes all persons in their relations to one another and to their common ends. The chief weakness of the modern Platonic "religion of culture," is that its devotees put the true, the good, and the beautiful on a pedestal and worship them in abstraction from the concrete forms they take in the lives of scientists, good men, and artists. As a result, intrinsic values are cut off from their meaning for personal life, as well as from their implications for social life. There is nobility in the disinterested pursuit of universal ends such as truth or beauty. In a sense we must say that "art is for art's sake," i.e., for beauty's sake; that "goodness is its own reward," and the like. For these are intrinsic values and are loved for themselves or not at all. But an intrinsic value is not an impersonal value, that is, a quality that is related to persons merely in an accidental and external way. We have no notion whatever of an intrinsic value save as it fulfills and enhances a person and raises a community of persons to the level of spiritual dignity. This is the sense in which Professor Urban's definition of spirit in terms of "acknowledgment of values" should be taken.[5] It is not that the "trans-

[5] W. M. Urban, "Idealism and the Philosophy of Value," in *Contemporary Idealism in America* (ed., Clifford Barrett. New York, Macmillan, 1932).

THE ESSENCE OF SPIRIT

individual" and "trans-social" values to which he refers constitute an order of self-subsistent ideals or essences, by acknowledging which man raises himself to the dignity of spirit. For this would make spirit secondary to the absolute values it recognizes. Rather, spirit and the values it acknowledges imply one another. Spirit is prior in the order of efficient causes, value is prior in the order of final causes. As the efficient causality of spiritual activity and the final causality of intrinsic values thus imply one another, they are both aspects of concrete spiritual life. Therefore, the Platonic emphasis upon absolute values and the Christian emphasis upon persons do not exclude but demand one another. For the individual must both live the spiritual life as a member of a community of persons and acknowledge the absolute values which give dignity to their existence.

Moreover, the union of the individual with the universal need not be and usually is not an unmediated one. Individuality is broadened and enriched by participation in the wider life of the family, the church, the town, and the nation. Hence communities like these may be said to mediate the universal to the individual, widening the vision of the individual and specifying the universal in such a way as to make it more concrete and accessible. The danger of substituting loyalty to the smaller community for loyalty to the universal itself, for example, loyalty to the university, the church, or the state for loyalty to truth, religion, or the world community, should not blind us to this important fact. Devotion to these actual communities is not incompatible with devotion to the ideal community, so long as no actual community such as the state sets itself up as requiring an absolute loyalty. The main criticism of a theory of spirit which stresses devotion to the universal, namely, that it leads to neglect of the concrete manifestations of the universal in everyday life, is met in this way. The fact that the practical man who devotes himself to his family, his profession, or his town, may not always think of himself as serving the universal values of a community that is still largely ideal, means only that his vision of the wider bearings of his acts may be limited. Often excellent service is rendered to the universal by those who recognize it only as it shows itself in the particular person or concrete situation before them.

Now, the universal community devoted to absolute values is at any given time partly an ideal, partly an actuality. It is in process of coming to be. This leads us to the third attribute of spirit, its *creativity*. The spirit finds itself in a world which is in large part foreign to it and its ideals, but which may be transformed by its creative action. We have seen how Plato's inadequate conception of will and his static conception of reality led him to treat creation as the mere imposition of a universal pattern upon a given particular matter. Under the influence of Christianity and of modern dynamic conceptions, however, we have come to realize that it is only through a process of interaction between the creative agent and the material at his disposal that a form can be conceived and realized which will express both the purpose of the one and the potentiality of the other. This may be true of the creation of the cosmos by God, no less than of the creation of a work of art or a just city by men. God's creation may be not so much an arbitrary imposition of form upon matter which is wholly foreign to it, as a patient process by which forms suitable to the potencies of particular matters are realized. In some such way the working out of God's creative purposes, in relation to human beings at least, may have to be conceived if providence is not to swallow up freedom. But whatever may be true of divine creation, human creation is surely of this sort. In art, the medium (matter of a certain sort) exercises an influence upon the artist, helping him to define his intention more clearly as he works with it, and he does not know his intention fully until the process of realizing it in the medium is over.[6] Similarly, in political life the real statesman is not one who conceives a Utopia by abstracting from the imperfect actualities of his country and then imposes it upon

---

[6] See Samuel Alexander, *Art and the Material* (New York, Longmans, Green, 1925).

his fellow-citizens by military force or demagogic flattery. Rather, he is one who can see behind the actualities of his country greater possibilities than his fellows see and can lead them by a minimum of force and a maximum of persuasion to adopt policies which will realize these. Spirit creates, in part by imposing form from without, but also by transforming from within.

It is at this point that Hegel's conception of spirit shows its most profound insight: spirit can find and realize itself only in and through that which is other than itself. It must overcome the otherness of that which is external to itself by penetrating it with meaning. Hegel's view that the objective will always be found to be itself ultimately spiritual, spirit within meeting spirit without, does not seem to me essential to this insight. Indeed, it seems to me to weaken it. For spiritual activity is capable of transforming precisely that which is not spiritual until it takes on spiritual significance. In art, for example, a sensuous object can take on form and express a universal idea. In society, subjective freedom can make itself effective through objective laws and institutions. Everywhere the spirit finds itself by transforming precisely that which in itself is foreign to it. Moreover, the spirit's creative work must not be stopped by an optimistic view of things as they are, for its transformation of that which is opposed to it is far from perfect. This is the truth

THE ESSENCE OF SPIRIT

which lies behind the Christian conception of the Kingdom of God as "coming," for the Kingdom is an ideal which can be approximated but never wholly realized under the conditions of finite existence.

Creativity implies *freedom*. For freedom is spontaneity, determination from within. Now the freedom of the spirit is intelligible only in relation to its activity in realizing universal ends. Berdyaev's failure to stress this seems to me to constitute the greatest weakness in his analysis of freedom.[7] To him freedom is not related to the "substantial nature" of a person. Rather he says: "It is rooted in non-being. Freedom is originally and entirely irrational."[8] The ground for this seems to be that reason can grasp only that which is static and substantial, while the spirit's freedom is dynamic, creative, and infinite in potentiality. But the effect is that freedom of the spirit is made to appear completely irrational, as if it were a sort of spiritual energy that arises out of nothing in us and therefore expresses nothing permanent in ourselves. Spontaneity, as it were, bubbles up as from a spring of cosmic life. Interpreted idealistically, as it is by Berdyaev, this logically leads to divine determinism or to romanticism. Interpreted naturalistically, it might easily degenerate into a theory of Dionysian urges rising out of the depths

[7] Nikolai Berdyaev, *Freedom and the Spirit* (New York, Charles Scribner's Sons, 1935).
[8] *Ibid.*, p. 124.

of nature. That way lies antinomianism, in which the guidance of free action by rational and moral principle disappears. The danger of such a conception in an age like ours when vitalistic ways of thinking threaten to submerge the categories distinctive of spiritual activity hardly needs to be pointed out. It is vividly illustrated by the use made of Gentile's dynamic spiritualism by the Fascists as a justification for their exaltation of arbitrary action by a leader or a state.

Indeed, as it is only reason which can apprehend universal truth and value, *rationality* must be regarded as a fourth attribute of spirit. It is the glory of Plato that he saw the importance, both for theory and practice, of the universal and of the reason which apprehends it. Unfortunately, Christianity was very slow in learning what Plato never doubted, that the spiritual life of the Kingdom must be, in the broad sense of the term, a rational life.[9] There were several historical reasons for this. Christianity was born into the Graeco-Roman world at a time when trust in reason was rapidly decaying. Its distinctive genius lay in a deepened moral insight and religious feeling, rather than in a passion for truth in all its forms. Shortly after it finally conquered the Roman

---

[9] I do not, of course, mean that rationality must be present in the same degree or form in all persons; nor that by itself it constitutes a person spiritual; nor that the poet's intuition and the prophet's faith should be scorned by the rational person. I believe that there is a kind of intuition charged with emotion which is in its essence rational.

THE ESSENCE OF SPIRIT 57

Empire, barbarian invasions threatened the very existence of the classical learning. St. Augustine's brilliant use of his learning to defend pessimistic doctrines of original sin and predestination showed how impossible it was in a dying world for reason to be free. Yet Christianity had begun to assimilate the best Greek thought from New Testament times; there was a strong school of Christian Platonists in Alexandria in the second and third centuries; and in the Middle Ages most of the best thinkers could not tolerate the idea that faith was contrary to reason. From the beginning, therefore, it has been obvious to the most thoughtful minds that Christianity is not hostile to reason as such, but only to what St. Paul called the "wisdom of this world."

It is interesting to note that Christianity has not been alone in its war upon false or narrow conceptions of reason. The abstract rationalism of the Age of Enlightenment provoked a vigorous reaction on the part of romantic poets like Wordsworth and Coleridge. For reason had come to be identified by many with the analytical and critical faculty which gave rise to modern materialism and positivism. The romantic reaction gave way to the naturalism of the later nineteenth century, a naturalism which was enormously strengthened by new theories in biology and psychology. Reason was restricted to scientific analysis of and inference from objects of sense. Religion, which had still found it possible to appeal to reason in the eighteenth century, was forced more and more to resort to faith and feeling. As a result, there developed a sharp dualism between head and heart, reason and faith, science and poetry, a dualism which has plagued the best minds of the post-Darwinian period. I regard this dualism as the greatest tragedy of modern thought, and I believe the blame for it falls squarely upon those who have been blind to the higher function of reason.

What is this higher function? Whereas practical intelligence is employed primarily for biological and utilitarian ends, there is a faculty of intellect which is disinterested. Whereas science may limit itself to the analysis and description of phenomena and their relations, there is a faculty of intellect which thinks them synoptically as wholes and penetrates to their essence by intuition. It will not do, of course, to oppose this synoptic and intuitive faculty to the scientific intellect. For the analysis of phenomena often leads the reflective scientist into speculation concerning their togetherness and deeper meaning. The scientist may also be a philosopher and a poet, though he is often too modest or too proud to admit the fact. On the other hand, the synopsis and intuition of the philosopher and poet are of little value unless they rest upon patient analysis and observation in an objective spirit. Thus, the data with which the scientist deals, far from being beneath the dignity of the philosophic or poetic faculty, are absolutely essential to it. But the work of the exact scientist also needs to be supplemented by the philosopher and the poet. The knowledge of matter of fact, even when it takes the form of scientific laws, is not the final aim of the intellect. This is shown by the tendency of scientists like Whitehead to become philosophers and of scientists like Einstein to formulate all-embracing hypotheses from which the principles of special fields can be deduced.

In other words, intellect at the highest level, whether exercised by scientist, philosopher or poet, is inspired by a passion for ultimate reality and value. Hence, Plato was not wrong in making the distinguishing character of pure intellect its interest in the metaphysical foundation of all specialized knowledge, and insisting that this ultimate reality must be viewed under the aspect of absolute value ("the Idea of the Good"). Of course, curiosity, cleverness, and acuteness of intelligence may be possessed in high degree by men with no passion for ultimate reality and absolute goodness. But pure intellect is fully actualized only in those who seek to know reality and through knowing to become one with its goodness. Pure intellect seeks the ultimate ground of all existence and value, in order to come to terms with that upon which everything is dependent. In this respect, philosophy, religion, and poetry at their best are one; for in their different ways they seek to wed insight into truth with love of the goodness truth reveals.

Finally, spirit is *love* born of faith and objectivity. Spirit does not prize itself; it prizes that which is objective to itself. This insight is, we saw, derived primarily from Christianity. But the nature of Christian love is so often misunderstood that it is necessary to analyze its meaning further. We shall not concern ourselves with the theological basis of brotherly love, namely, the prior love of God for men. What we must notice is the general character of brotherly love. In the first place, it does not rest primarily upon natural sentiment and sympathy, upon the sort of affinity which draws together the members of a family or a nation. Since one's "neighbor" or one's "brother" is anyone whose life touches one's own, whatever his class or race,[10] love for him must issue from a settled disposition or will rather than a sporadic feeling. In the second place, this disposition is more than general "benevolence" or "good will" in the ordinary sense; it involves understanding, insight into the nature and needs of men. For this a generalized knowledge of human nature derived from broad experience or from social and psychological science is not enough; one must have the sort of understanding of one's neighbor that comes only by sympathetic and sometimes painful identification with him as a unique individual.

[10] As is made clear by the parable of the good Samaritan.

In the third place, love of neighbor expresses itself in practical acts which serve his needs, indeed, in an affirmation of his whole being. Thus brotherly love is intensely practical and positive.

Moreover, the quality of brotherly love is affected deeply by the wider perspective provided by Christian belief, especially belief concerning the nature and good of man. Man is a son of God, made in the divine image; and he is called to a perfection like that of his Father. Therefore, brotherly love must not overlook the divine potentialities of the person loved, as if there were nothing more in him than his empirical character. He is not to be loved according to his merit in human eyes, but according to his worth in the sight of God. We are not to love him simply for his good qualities or for his friendliness to us. For love is not to be calculated as if it were something to mete out justly in different degrees to different persons; rather, it is to be poured out without measure. We must not love or withdraw love according as it is or is not merited or returned. The generosity of our love will be attested by our ability to love even our enemies and to forgive again and again those who wrong us. Love like this is obviously based upon something more than understanding of and sympathy with one's neighbor as he actually is. It is based upon faith in him as he might be and desire to love him as God loves him. Its practice, therefore, requires a restraint of egoistic impulses which to the worldly has always seemed impossible.

There is a further point of great importance. Brotherly love is not content with affirming the good of one's neighbor as an individual; rather it relates the good of one's neighbor to the ideal community of all men, the Kingdom of God. The Christian loves his neighbor as he is and might be, considered as an individual; but he loves him also as a potential member of the universal community which is to be built upon the principle of love. He cannot love him as he ought without desiring that he should be a member of this community. Thus, Christian love is for the individual, but in the light of the universal. As a result it avoids the opposite errors of Platonism and individualism. On the Platonic theory, love is directed to that in the individual which is universal. On the theory of modern individualism, it is the individual by and for himself alone who is loved. But the Christian loves the person as an individual member of the universal community.

If it is dangerous to neglect either the individual uniqueness of one's neighbor or his relation to the universal end, it is equally dangerous to separate them sharply from each other. One of the most interesting analyses of love in recent philosophy, that of Hartmann, is vitiated by this error.[11] "Brotherly

[11] Nicolai Hartmann, *Ethics* (trans., Stanton Coit. London, G. Allen & Unwin, 1932), Vol. II.

love" (or "love of neighbor") and "love of the remote" are conceived by him as so antithetical that he is unable to bring them into fruitful relation with one another. One reason for this is to be found in his almost exclusive use of the analytical method. His use of analysis to separate completely three different kinds of love ("brotherly love," "love of the remote," and "personal love") leads him to find irreconcilable "antinomies" where there are only distinctions, "essences" opposed to one another where there are only aspects closely related to one another.

But the main reason is that Hartmann's conception of both "brotherly love" and "love of the remote" is inadequate. He recognizes the "positive affirmative tendency" of brotherly love, the necessity for a deep intuitive understanding of the loved one, and the intimacy and richness of the personal relationship with him. He also recognizes that, though brotherly love is love of neighbor, potentially every human being is a neighbor; and he can even envisage a time when love of neighbor may be so extended as to exercise a great power over human destiny. Despite this, however, Hartmann shares part of Nietzsche's view of brotherly love. It is "an every-day virtue," as love of the remote is "an exceptional one," he says.[12] It is easy, while love of the remote is hard. It is leveling in its effect, because it considers the need rather than the merit of the

[12] *Ibid.*, p. 329 n.

neighbor. Thus, it seeks the welfare of everyone, bringing into play no selective principle to favor those most likely to improve the race. For this and other reasons, love of the remote "requires an overcoming of one's commitment to the nearest," the ethos of brotherly love must "retire into the background and give way to another ethos."[13]

"Love of the remote," on the other hand, is love of the ideal humanity of the future. But if we are to serve the future well, it seems we must be willing to subordinate or overcome our commitments to those who are nearest to us. For love of the remote is opposed to the sympathetic leveling principle of brotherly love. "It must unearth again the principle of selection which love of the nearest has buried. It must reinstate the worthiest, the ethically strong and aspiring, and favour him at the cost of the man who is sinking."[14] Hartmann realizes the danger that this may lead to cruelty, to a wanton sacrifice of the present to the future. He guards against this by pointing out that men have no right to treat others *merely* as means to the end of an ideal future. But the antinomy remains. If we are not to avoid our responsibility to the future, brotherly love must be limited. Those who are noble and great of spirit must transcend the altruism of brotherly love for the sake of the ideal humanity of the future.

Now, this sharp separation of "love of the near-

[13] *Ibid.*, p. 318.   [14] *Ibid.*, p. 319.

est" and "love of the furthest" does violence to both, depriving the former of all reference to the ultimate ideal and the latter of all contact with the reality of the here and now. It is, of course, possible to love one's neighbor with little vision of an ideal good of any kind for him. But to identify such a love with Christian love of neighbor, as Hartmann does, is to caricature the latter. As we pointed out above, Christian love is not directed towards the empirical character of the individual alone but takes into account also his ideal character as a son of God and a potential member of the universal community. To deny or minimize this ideal and universal reference of Christian love is to confuse it with natural affection or sympathy. That way lies individualism, which neglects the spiritual nature of one's neighbor and even abstracts from his social relations.

The futurism of Hartmann's "love of the remote" is equally erroneous. It represents the tendency of modern humanitarianism and evolutionism to substitute a religion of progress for the noble ideal of a universal community of love. It is true that one *can* love the ideal future of humanity at the cost of brotherly love for the actual persons one sees around one. But to say that this futuristic love represents the norm for our attitude towards either future or present is fallacious. Any ideal for the remote future which emphasizes its radical difference from the present is bound to be abstract if not empty.

Any construction of such an ideal is largely problematical. It is likely to seem fantastic, as Nietzsche's Superman does to most of us. But even if the ideal were perfectly clear and consistent, we would not be justified in "overcoming" or even "limiting" brotherly love for the sake of it. Brotherly love, as we have analyzed it, is an essential part of any legitimate ideal for the future. Any ideal, such as that of German National Socialism, which requires its denial or limitation is *ipso facto* a false ideal. In practice such an ideal would lead to, always has led to, a contempt for and sacrifice of concrete flesh-and-blood persons, not by ones and twos but by thousands. The danger of making the present a mere steppingstone to a splendid but Utopian future is vividly illustrated by the willingness of Communists to tolerate any amount of cruelty and injustice under the "dictatorship of the proletariat" in the naïve faith that it will bring about the "classless society" in a more or less remote future. By contrast, we must reassert the Christian conception of brotherly love: an habitual disposition to affirm the good of each person as understanding of his unique nature and faith in his spiritual potentiality reveal it.

Finally, it is obvious that men cannot attain to spiritual life in its perfection. For though a person may be transformed by spirit and brought under the service of its higher ends, yet the way is hard and beset with distractions. Man is a mixed creature, a microcosm containing in himself all the kinds and levels of being in the macrocosm. The Scholastics conceived of him as a creature rooted in nature by the materiality of his body and the limitations of his mind, yet tending towards the spiritual life by his essence as a son of God. Man is not a spirit, he is a composite of matter and spirit. He is an embodied soul trying to attain to the dignity of a spiritual person. But he is held back at every turn: by the weakness of his aspiration, by the willfulness of his private self, by the loss through worldliness of his vision of universal good. That is why discipline is necessary for the spiritual life. That is why the spiritual life in its purity is so rare to find and slow to win. That, finally, is why the spiritual life often seems so tragic. It is defeated time and again, in individual and society alike; and there are whole periods when it appears to be almost submerged.

> Man is of dust: ethereal hopes are his,
> Which, when they should sustain themselves aloft,
> Want due consistence; like a pillar of smoke,
> That with majestic energy from earth
> Rises; but, having reached the thinner air,
> Melts, and dissolves, and is no longer seen.[15]

It is, therefore, a romantic exaggeration to say, with Hegel, that the spirit is in all that all men think and do, and that every state and culture represents the Divine Idea on earth. But there is an important

[15] William Wordsworth, *The Excursion*, Book IV, ll. 140-45.

truth behind this exaggeration: for all men are called to raise their personal and common life to the level of spirit. They never quite succeed, but they are never quite able to forget their vocation. The opposite view, that of our modern naturalists and Marxists, is that spirit is an appearance or a by-product of that which is not spirit. This view is worse than false, it is an insult to human nature. The only grain of truth it contains is that men will not and cannot see spirit when they are busy looking at other things. Somewhere between the romantic affirmation of spirit everywhere and the cynical denial of its importance anywhere is the more subtle error of those who say that spirit exists in man but that it is impotent and irrelevant to the practical concerns of human life, to artistic creation, to moral decision, to political action. But to affirm the *reality* of spirit, and then to deny its *power* to transform any person who follows its lead, is a paradox which can appeal only to those who have known its shadow without its substance. As a creative activity of persons, spirit has *power*. That is the faith of high religion; and it is confirmed by our actual experience of spirit as a creative force in human life.

CHAPTER III

FREEDOM AND THE SPIRIT

SPIRIT IS THE creative activity by which persons apprehend universal truth and good with rational insight and serve men with love born of faith in their divine potentialities. That was the general result of our analysis of spirit. As we saw, creative activity of this kind involves freedom. But a closer analysis is required if we are to give concrete meaning to freedom. Such an analysis must take into account the fact that the spirit must exercise its freedom in relation to the opportunities afforded and the limitations imposed by the objective world. If its creativity is to transform the world which surrounds it, it must be able to embody subjective decisions in objective reality. Its capacity to do so is the measure of its power, its causal efficacy. If it has no effective freedom, it has no real power. It becomes an accidental by-product of natural forces, always an effect and never a cause. In short, the appearance of its creativity becomes a sheer illusion. Modern materialists, economic determinists, and political realists accept this view of spirit as an epiphenomenal by-product and powerless spectator of natural events. Have we anything to say in reply to their view? The issue is not an academic one. If belief in the freedom and power of the spirit fails, as it seems to be failing in many European nations, the whole of Western culture will be endangered and a new barbarism will threaten us.

This would be the more tragic because the human spirit has taken more than two thousand years to attain a full understanding of its freedom. Hegel is so impressed with the importance of this slow and painful process that he conceives of the history of the world as "none other than the progress of the consciousness of freedom." The Orientals, he says, never attained the knowledge that man as such is free but only that *one* man is free and free in the capricious manner of the despot. The Greeks first developed the consciousness of freedom but they knew only that *some* are free and thought that most men have to be slaves. Under the influence of Christianity, the Western peoples came to know that *man* as man is free because he is a spiritual being. "But to introduce the principle into the various relations of the actual world, involves a more extensive problem than its simple implantation (as an ideal); a problem whose solution and application require a severe and lengthened process of culture."[1] He illustrates the point by reference to the slowness of the processes by which slavery was abolished and political liberty attained among Western peoples. Hegel's penetrating insight may be taken as the starting point for an historical analysis of the idea of freedom. If we can realize how hardly and painfully men have come to understand the complex nature and conditions of their freedom, we may see more clearly the sacrifice we make when we surrender it, or any part of it, in thought or in deed.

We will begin with a brief reference to Plato's thought, though on this point especially he is representative of the limitation rather than the strength of the Greek genius. It has been said that Plato sacrifices freedom to order in his Republic. This is, of course, an exaggeration, but there is much truth in it. The slaves are not even regarded as members of the city-state. The workers and farmers, who form the base of the social pyramid and constitute the majority of the citizens, are denied the right to participate in government. They are to have instilled in them the virtue of temperance in their private, and obedience in their public, lives. In return, they are to be given just rule and protection by the ruling classes while they perform their function as producers of food and goods for the city.

[1] G. W. F. Hegel, *Lectures on the Philosophy of History* (trans., J. Sibree. London, H. G. Bohn, 1861), pp. 360, 361.

They will be allowed to marry, make money, and enjoy what private happiness they can. But they will have neither intellectual nor political liberty; they must think and do what they are told.

The class of soldiers occupies a position between the producers and the rulers. As their whole life must be devoted to the protection of the city, they can neither marry nor engage in business.[2] They are to possess courage, a high civic virtue, and they will take pride in being the watchdogs of the city. Moreover, though they will not help to decide upon matters of political policy, they will be given an education which will furnish them with true opinions and thus enable them to know why they must do what the rulers command. Thus, the soldiers have a degree of freedom since blind obedience is not required of them in the performance of their function; and they are granted a limited participation in public affairs as auxiliaries of the rulers.

But it is only the small class of rulers or governors who have what we should regard as full freedom. They, and they alone, are free to investigate scientific truth and thus attain to the knowledge that is complete virtue. They and they alone are free to deliberate and decide upon the laws of the city. They are related to the other two classes, especially the first, as rulers to ruled, artists in statecraft to the human material upon which they are to impose

---

[2] That is to say, their wives and property will be in common.

form. Plato seems to be almost blind to the potential rationality and responsibility of the many. The freedom encouraged by democracy is to him identical with anarchy, and the ideal republic of which he dreams is aristocratic and authoritarian.

It must not be thought that Plato's restriction of intellectual and political freedom to a small group of wise rulers represents a preference on his part for tyranny. He shares completely the Greek hatred of arbitrary government by tyrants. But he thinks that government by a group of wise and virtuous men would be superior to oligarchy or democracy or tyranny since it would be exercised in the interest of all classes in the state rather than of the few rich or the many poor or the rulers themselves. It is not, then, that he rejects freedom; it is rather that he does not see that political, intellectual, and cultural freedom are necessary or expedient for the happiness of the many. That is why Plato is so significant for an understanding of Greek thought on freedom after the belief in democracy had begun to decline. Aristotle is perhaps equally significant. For, despite his qualified defense of democracy against the criticisms of aristocrats, he excludes slaves and resident aliens from citizenship, limits very narrowly the participation of workers and farmers in public affairs, and takes it for granted that the state will control the moral education and the religious practice of its citizens. The truth is, the conception of the worth of the individual and the recognition of certain rights as necessary to the effective exercise of his freedom are not characteristic of the two greatest Greek thinkers.

It was Christianity which was mainly responsible for the recognition that all men have intrinsic worth. The Christian view that all men are sons of God, irrespective of race, religion, or class, was a charter of freedom to oppressed groups. Women and children could now be treated as persons, with lives of their own, and slaves could be regarded as equal to their masters, at least in the sight of God. These principles, for a number of reasons, were prevented from revolutionizing all the relations of men in the late Roman Empire and the medieval period. The deep-rooted habits of the pagan world, the invasions of the barbarians, the rise of the feudal system with its rigid social structure, and the hierarchical organization of the church were among these conditions. As a result, intellectual and political freedom was very limited in the lower orders of society and the principle of authority was supreme.

On the other hand, early and medieval Christians were greatly interested in moral freedom, and made keen analyses of its roots in the reason and the will. The strength of Aristotle's theory of choice following rational deliberation lay in the implied distinction between natural desire and deliberate choice, a distinction which provided the basis for a theory of rational will. Christian thinkers insisted that the will, unlike natural desire, could act or withhold its act, in short, that it could determine itself from within. This freedom of the will could be conceived in either of two ways. In the first place, it could be identified with the determination of acts by reason. This rationalistic view keeps freedom from being confused with the blind impulsiveness of animal appetite. Its weakness is that it makes freedom a property of reason rather than of will. In the second place, it could be identified, as by Duns Scotus, with the indifference of the will between competing alternatives, even after these alternatives have been weighed by reason. "Freedom is therefore wholly centred in the radical indetermination of the will, whose unforeseeable decisions spring from within as from a source of determinations wholly undetermined by anything else."[3] Such a voluntaristic view takes spontaneity seriously and locates it in the will as the source of actions. But it tends to make rational deliberation useless and to reduce will once more to impulse. Hence, Aquinas attempted to synthesize the one-sided theories of the rationalists and the voluntarists by maintaining that "choice is essentially an act of the *will*" but that "without the *judgment* will would not be will." The issue is interesting chiefly because of the light it throws upon the way in which philosophers sought

[3] Étienne Gilson, *The Spirit of Medieval Philosophy*, p. 310.

to emphasize the Christian belief in the initiative of moral will without giving up the Greek belief in the primary importance of reason. They see clearly both that will is quite different from natural desire and that its freedom depends upon the rational nature of man.

The other issue which exercised early and medieval Christians is even more illuminating. It rests upon the distinction between freedom to choose and freedom to effect. It is of no avail that the will is free, they argued, if it has no power to use its freedom well. Through original sin the will has been corrupted to its very depths. Freedom in the sense of choice remains a part of the nature of will, but freedom in the sense of power to do right has been lost. Hence, God's grace is indispensable if this power is to be restored. From Augustine onwards, therefore, "real" freedom was regarded as a gift of divine grace which heals the will and strengthens it to do right. Gilson puts the argument of Anselm in this way: "The real power [of will] is the power of efficaciously willing the good; having done evil, the will remains free to will the good, but not to do it; it is therefore but a wounded liberty; in restoring the lost power grace restores to free-will something of its first efficacy; far from diminishing it, it liberates it."[4] The double assumption behind this argument is that "real" freedom implies the power to do right

[4] *Ibid.*, p. 318.

and that this power has been lost by original sin. From this double assumption it is a short step to the conclusion that the divine grace by which men are prevented from sinning does not destroy but rather restores their freedom.[5] If will depends upon reason for guidance, argued Aquinas, the more infallible the reason is made by God's grace, the more liberty there is in the will.[6]

The danger of this doctrine that divine determinism insures freedom is obvious. Logically, its assumption of the corruption of human will would paralyze the confidence of Christians in themselves and lead to complete dependence upon divine grace as the source of all improvement. Hence, the Church, which as the ark of salvation has in its keeping the instruments of divine grace, should control the conscience of men. Also, the utter dependence of all men upon this divine grace would tend to discourage attempts at reform in the economic and political spheres. The subjection of moral and religious freedom to the Church was in fact paralleled by the subjection of economic and political freedom to the feudal system. As a result, the noble conception of man as a son of God free to devote his will creatively to the furthering of the Kingdom was

[5] For an acute criticism of the doctrine of irresistible grace and its negation of moral freedom and for a defense of a more reasonable doctrine of grace, see John Oman, *Grace and Personality* (2nd ed. Cambridge, Cambridge University Press, 1919).

[6] Gilson, *op. cit.*, p. 321.

rendered ineffective and in practice men obeyed spiritual and temporal authority in every sphere of life.[7]

Of course, political and economic conditions had played a large part in the restriction of effective freedom by the Greek philosopher and the Christian theologian. It need not surprise us, therefore, that men had to wait for a full vindication of their freedom—moral, religious, political, and economic—until the Protestant reformers, absolute monarchs, and new bourgeoisie destroyed the authority of the ecclesiastical hierarchy and the power of the feudal lords. Only then was freedom able to assert itself decisively both in the inner and in the outer spheres. Kant gives the clearest expression to the modern belief in *inner* freedom as it finally developed in the eighteenth century. By his insistence upon the autonomy of the moral will in laying down laws for its own actions he vindicates freedom as essential to morality. Thus, at a stroke he frees morality from ecclesiastical and political authority and rests it upon personal responsibility. Kant makes it clear, however, that the individual's moral autonomy has nothing to do with his natural or enlightened self-interest, but requires his submission to universal moral laws which take no account of his inclinations. In this

[7] This is not to deny that the best medieval thinkers such as Aquinas sought in their economic and political theory to defend men against arbitrary oppression and tyranny.

way, he binds together moral freedom with responsibility. Equally important, he insists upon the intrinsic worth and dignity of persons as rational beings. They are ends-in-themselves and as such must be permitted to determine their ends for themselves. That is what justifies the system of rights enforced by law in the state, for it protects the freedom of men and makes them respect the freedom of others. This may not be democracy, but it is the moral charter of democracy. For true democracy is possible only where men both assert their rights and respect the rights of others as moral persons.

Unfortunately, the formalism of the moral law as Kant conceives it would logically tend to make the actual exercise of moral freedom ineffective. For in order that the moral law may be laid down by reason absolutely and universally, Kant says, it must take account neither of human nature nor of the consequences of the will's acts. In short, reason must, independently of all experience, draw forth moral imperatives by some miracle out of itself. But how can there be any assurance that such imperatives will correspond to the nature and needs of men in a particular society at a particular time? Moreover, what is to prevent imperatives laid down by abstract reason in this fashion from becoming in practice arbitrary and subjective? May not personal prejudices be taken for universal laws? In other words, moral autonomy, when exercised by reason in such an abstract way, may lay down moral imperatives which are either irrelevant or arbitrary.

Moreover, Kant holds that freedom belongs to the "transcendental" self but not to the "empirical" self. The acts we perform as empirical selves, together with the consequences of these acts, fall under the sway of natural laws. Thus a dualism is set up within the self, and subjective freedom is divorced from objective effectiveness. This, in turn, may lead to a divorce between ethics and politics, the former confining itself to personal rectitude and leaving to the latter all decisions concerning actions insofar as they have social consequences. On this view, one and the same person might be righteous in his personal, but ruthless in his public, life.

Meanwhile, lesser thinkers than Kant fell into an individualistic and rationalistic interpretation of freedom in the *outer* sphere that led to equally dangerous theories. The eighteenth-century revolutionary thinkers of France and England were insisting, in the name of reason, upon certain "natural rights" for all men without regard to historical or social circumstances. Burke's attack upon these thinkers is instructive.[8] It is foolish, he says, to exalt the "natural rights" conceived by abstract reason above the "civil rights" guaranteed by the laws and customs of England. An alleged "natural right" can never be granted by society in its pure, abstract form; it can

[8] *Reflections on the Revolution in France.*

be admitted only insofar as it is expedient for society as a whole. It will not do, therefore, to praise any and every kind of freedom; one must inquire into the capacity of men of a given class and time to exercise it, its consequences for law and order, and the limitations to be placed upon its exercise. In short, the question whether a political right or privilege should be granted can never be decided by appealing to a supposed rational claim of all men to it but only by determining its expediency for a given society. Now, every society recognizes civil and political rights which have grown up naturally in the course of its history. It is more important to guard and cherish these old rights which have been received as inheritances from the fathers than to claim new ones. Moreover, the granting of rights must be limited by the political institutions and social classes which exist in the given society. Certain rights belong to aristocracy as aristocracy, to clergy as clergy, to property-holders as property-holders; and those rights must neither be destroyed nor usurped by cobblers and weavers. Rights are not equally the privileges of all citizens, but are relative to their status and function.

On Burke's view, then, rights are to be determined, not by abstract reason, but by empirical considerations of general expediency, historical tradition, and class status. The contrast with Kant is striking. Whereas Kant exalts the freedom of the moral will,

Burke is concerned primarily with the concrete liberties guaranteed by the state. Kant sees that without moral freedom a man can do nothing he ought to do; Burke insists that a man must exercise his liberty within the limits imposed by his status and by the form and tradition of society. He does not possess an independent and unconditioned will, which lays down universal laws in an abstract manner; he is a citizen of a community with a long history and his decisions must be made accordingly. In short, Kant is content with nothing short of universals and absolutes, while Burke is a historical thinker who is at home only with the particulars and relativities of time and place. But is it necessary, we ask, that absolute and relative, universal and particular, be regarded as incompatible? May it not be that universal norms are essential to moral responsibility but that they must be applied in political action with a full recognition of the realities of a particular time and place?

Now Hegel's doctrine of freedom may be treated as an attempt to *synthesize* the claims of moral freedom stressed by Kant with the requirements of political solidarity stressed by conservatives like Burke, with chief emphasis upon the latter. The key to Hegel's synthesis lies in his view of the relation between the subjective and objective aspects of morality. The fundamental defect of Kant's moral theory, he thinks, is his opposition of the moral subject and his freedom to the objective world and its necessity. This leads to a formal and unreal freedom, the will being regarded as free in its acts whether its concrete ends are attained or not. The result is that the will tends to withhold action in the objective sphere and to withdraw into a private world of scrupulous but impotent moral rectitude. In a passive nature, such a moral subjectivism leads to flight from an evil world; in an active and restless one, it produces the temper of the revolutionary who censures and wishes to destroy the existing order because he does not find it perfect.

The only way to avoid this, Hegel thinks, is to refuse to set up our subjective ideals of right and justice as superior to the social system of right and justice under which we live. Rather, if we would translate our subjective freedom into objective effectiveness, must we affirm the solid social realities around us. This means that we must be loyal citizens of the state. The state is no mere political organization which maintains external order by force, it is the supreme embodiment of the spirit of a people. Its customs, its laws, its institutions, are products of their rationality. It is not an alien irrational power standing over against the citizen and limiting his freedom; it is the objectification of his own higher will, it is what he freely wills when he is rational. It is only his caprice, not his freedom, which is constrained by it. It is his own moral substance, since he participates through habit and feeling in its common life. Even his moral duty is determined by his position in the state; and his duty, far from limiting his freedom, expresses it. As Hegel puts it, "What a man ought to do . . . is in an ethical community not hard to say. He has to do nothing except what is presented, expressed and recognized in his established relations."[9]

Thus Hegel, beginning with the obvious truth that subjective freedom must be made effective in the objective world, ends by requiring the individual to subordinate his will and even his conscience to the state. Hegel seems to have thought that he was saving freedom, which he regarded as constituting the "substantial and essential character of the will." Subjective freedom, he argued, can be reconciled with the necessity of absolute obedience, for the state is a "concrete universal" including the individual as an integral part of itself. Moreover, the state is not merely the government, it is society as organized into institutions, classes, and professions the members of each of which contribute to the life of the whole in a way peculiar to themselves. But though Hegel intended in this way to preserve the freedom of individuals and associations as organs of the state, there is not much doubt that the tendency of his view is towards political absolutism. It is not only that he

[9] *The Philosophy of Right* (trans., S. W. Dyde. London, G. Bell & Sons, 1896), p. 159.

scorns the eighteenth-century belief in natural rights and parliamentary democracy, it is that the unique worth of the individual in general is minimized while the state is exalted as "the Divine Idea on earth." Moreover, the duty of the citizen being defined by his position in the state, it can hardly be his duty to criticize the state in the name of the moral law; indeed, the state is regarded as the guardian of the whole moral and spiritual life.

However, there is a solid core of truth in Hegel's theory of freedom. Freedom must not be a mere subjective and arbitrary thing; it must be devoted to universal ends and purposes. Ideally, such devotion might be attained best by the identification of the individual with the common life of the society which has nourished him. If he could find his own highest ends and purposes already realized in social institutions, he might devote himself wholeheartedly to them as expressions of his own will. Unfortunately, this ideal is seldom found completely realized in actual states, despite Hegel's view that the real is the rational. The difficulty here, as in his general theory of spirit, is that Hegel's monism leads him to identify too easily the individual with the universal, the ideal with the real, and hence freedom with necessity.

The most notable fact about the nineteenth and early twentieth centuries, as far as the idea of freedom is concerned, has been the development side by side of theories of extreme individualism and extreme collectivism. Individualism has been represented best by Liberals like John Stuart Mill, collectivism by Communists like Karl Marx. Democracy is the form of government developed by the former, dictatorship that developed by the latter. But though dictatorship is opposed to every kind of democracy, I think it could be shown that it is a natural reaction against individualism and the kind of democracy which is based upon individualism. We shall discuss this political issue in the next chapter; here we shall confine ourselves to the problem of the freedom of the individual.

In his *Logic* Mill argues that the law of causality holds for human volitions as well as for physical events: "Given the motives which are present to an individual's mind, and given likewise the character and disposition of the individual, the manner in which he will act may be unerringly inferred." But, though the individual's action thus invariably follows from causes, he is not helpless before those causes. "He has, to a certain extent, a power to alter his character.... His character is formed by his circumstances ... but his own desire to mould it in a particular way, is one of these circumstances, and by no means one of the least influential."[10] Thus, his actions follow from causes, but those causes are,

[10] J. S. Mill, *A System of Logic* (8th ed. New York, Harper & Brothers, 1900), p. 524.

within limits, under his control. By introducing a desire different from those already in play, he can change his character. In other words, Mill is a determinist and he believes that men can do much to shape the characters of others by what we should call "conditioning" them. But he also believes in "self-culture" by a process of determining one's self. One side of Mill's Liberalism springs from this profound belief in the capacity of individuals to determine their own lives. For this belief obviously underlies his passionate defense of the right of individuals to exercise their powers with the minimum of restraint. Thus, he defends liberty of thought and discussion as the best way to unmask error and arrive at truth. He favors representative government on the ground that it is the best way of developing social intelligence and responsibility among the citizens. He pleads for the emancipation of women from the social, political and economic handicaps to which they have been subjected. The major assumption of his treatises on these subjects is that men and women can be trusted to use their liberties in such a way as to benefit both themselves and others. Though such a defense of liberties is both too individualistic and too optimistic in its view of human nature for our post-war age, it represents the authentic aspirations of nineteenth-century Liberalism at its best. If the individual has high potentialities, these potentialities can be brought to fulfillment only with the help of religious, intellectual, and political liberties. This is the theme of the Liberalism developed in a less individualistic but more positive manner by men like T. H. Green[11] towards the end of the century.

But there is another side of Mill's doctrine which represents the great weakness of nineteenth-century Liberalism. I refer to his conception of the self and its good. His psychology was that of the eighteenth-century associationists as expounded by his father. The essence of the associationist psychology was its exclusive use of the analytical method, for an atomistic view of the mind resulted from that method. The mind was analyzed into a series of separate and distinct sensations, feelings, ideas, and volitions, related externally by laws of association. Its unity and identity were regarded as secondary, if not fictitious. As it had no permanent center of initiative within itself, it was regarded as largely dependent upon its natural and social environment for its character and contents. In other words, it was passive and plastic in relation to its environment. This view of the mind was used by the early Liberals to justify their boundless faith in the progress of men towards perfection. It led them to believe that the evils which afflict men were due almost wholly to social institutions, and encouraged them to hope for unlimited improvement once these institutions were reformed.

[11] *Lectures on the Principles of Political Obligation* (London, Longmans, Green, 1895).

Thus, the atomistic view of the self dissolves its unity into a series of conscious states and puts it at the mercy of its environment. Its unity lost, the self as a whole can no longer be logically regarded as the original source of its own acts. Will, the initiative of the self, disappears. Reliance is placed, not upon the initiative and responsibility of individual wills, but upon external reforms, as the primary condition of improvement. The freedom of individuals as creative agents inevitably falls into the background. Freedom in the sense of external opportunity takes its place, until freedom comes to be identified with the various liberties, privileges, or rights granted by society to the citizen. Each of these helps to fulfill a particular interest of the self, for example, the economic or political or intellectual interest, rather than the personality as a whole. Indeed, the idea of man as a moral personality tends to fall into the background, and in its stead there appears the idea of a complex of more or less related interests and experiences. This tendency, moreover, is closely associated with and strengthened by the utilitarian theory of human good as a series of pleasures rather than the fulfillment of a unitary self.

I would be the last to deny the immense value of the early Liberals' insistence upon external opportunities to make freedom effective; indeed I regard it as the most significant contribution of the nineteenth century to the concept of freedom. Nevertheless, I am convinced that Carlyle's attack upon the atomism, the utilitarianism, and the externalism of the Liberals of his day was fundamentally sound. You are giving men freedom of speech and assembly, he says, but what are you doing to guard against yellow journals and ranting demagogues? You are putting ballots into people's hands; but what are you doing to prevent their sale to the highest bidder? In short you are opening up many opportunities; are you providing any moral discipline for the responsible use of them? Moreover, is not your attempt to make men happy by multiplying their opportunities for satisfaction very one-sided? Is there not an infinite aspiration in men's souls which can be filled only by something worthy of loyalty and devotion? What universal ends and noble causes are you offering them? What are you giving them to work and sacrifice for?

But the attack of the Marxists upon the earlier Liberalism provides the most instructive commentary upon its weaker side. The Marxist doctrine of liberty rests upon the view that man is primarily a social and economic animal. The political, intellectual, and spiritual life is definitely secondary to, and conditioned by, the system of production. Hence, the liberty that counts most is economic opportunity. Sometimes the Marxist seems to argue that no other kind of liberty is worth talking about, at least until economic security has been attained

FREEDOM AND THE SPIRIT 91

by the masses. In short, for Mill's plurality of liberties, he substitutes economic liberty. Then he interprets economic liberty as economic security and puts up with the denial of all other liberties in order to attain it. Of course, he dreams of a classless society in which the state will have withered away and there will be the minimum of external restraint upon individuals. But during the transitional period before the classless society is reached, he allows the whole of life to be organized by an absolute government under the dictatorship of the proletariat or of the bureaucratic minority who claim to speak for them. This view is, of course, the negation of the best side of Liberalism, for it submerges the individual and his freedom in the mass and subjects him to dictatorial control in every department of his life. Thus, Marxism, lacking the earlier Liberals' belief in the dignity of the individual, carries their externalism to its final conclusion. The self is lost in the mass and becomes wholly dependent upon the group for economic security and culture. As economic security is the primary concern, political, intellectual, and religious liberties are sacrificed to an autocratic state which can organize most efficiently the production and distribution of material goods and culture.

But the disintegration of the Kantian concept of inner freedom and of the Liberal belief in liberties which support it was not the work of Marxian materialism alone. It was greatly accelerated by the biological and voluntaristic view of the mind to which the Darwinian theory of evolution seemed to lead. There are two interesting passages in Nietzsche which illustrate with brutal frankness the vitalistic conception of the will and its freedom. In *The Genealogy of Morals*[12] he pours scorn upon the "lambs," who, when they are attacked by the "birds of prey," think that the superior strength of the latter might be restrained by an act of will. The quantum of force which constitutes their will, he says, could not possibly be withheld from expressing itself. To argue as if it could is to assume wrongly that there is a *will behind* the force able to control its expression. In *Beyond Good and Evil*[13] he seems to deny altogether that thought and will belong to a personal agent. "I think" and "I will" are simply "fictions." "A thought comes when 'it' wishes, and not when I wish; so that it is a perversion of the facts of the case to say that the subject 'I' is the condition of the predicate 'think.' One thinks—one has even gone too far with this 'one thinks'—even the 'one' contains an *interpretation* of the process, and does not belong to the process itself." Freedom can be analyzed into muscular sensations, a dominant thought, an emotion of supremacy, and the like.

[12] (Trans., Horace B. Samuel. Edinburgh, J. N. Foulis, 1910), First essay, sec. 13.
[13] (Trans., Helen Zimmern. Edinburgh, J. N. Foulis, 1909), Chap. v, secs. 17-21.

The difference between a "free" and an "unfree" will is that the stronger will can command while the weaker can do nothing but obey. Thus in actuality it is not a question of free and unfree wills but of strong and weak wills. This theory would make of a person a mere channel through which impersonal vital forces flow. His thinking would become a process going on in him ("it thinks"), his willing, a stream of energy issuing from him. Contemporary expressions of the vitalistic theory of self and its freedom are not so harsh as that of Nietzsche. But one wonders whether the Nietzschean theory has not permeated the thought of many psychoanalysts and social psychologists more deeply than they themselves realize.

What conclusion can be derived from our analysis of the idea of freedom in Western thought? A brief summary may help us here. Plato saw clearly that something quite different from the satisfaction of animal appetite was needed for the fulfillment of rational beings. Thus, he laid the foundation for the theory that the highest freedom requires the mastery of reason over appetite. But he had no explicit theory of will; and he restricted the full application of his principle to the small class of wise rulers. The Christian thinkers of the Middle Ages went further: they developed a theory of will as free in its acts, though they disagreed as to whether its acts should be interpreted as rationally determined or as indifferent between alternatives. But though they deepened the understanding of the roots of freedom in the self, they were prevented by extreme doctrines of original sin and divine grace, from challenging the principle of secular and spiritual authority upon which medieval society rested. After the breakdown of that principle in the new national states and among the new middle classes of modern Europe, the full moral autonomy of men as rational beings could be asserted by Kant.[14] Unfortunately, Kant regarded that autonomy as belonging only to the transcendental self and as laying down purely formal and abstract laws for the will. The weakness of this view lay in its divorce of subjective freedom from objective effectiveness. Therefore, as Burke had criticized the natural rights claimed by abstract reason as inferior to the actual rights of the state which have been evolved during its history, Hegel now urged that subjective freedom is meaningless unless it identifies itself with the objective social institutions which alone can render freedom effective. But as Burke's view tends to conservatism by glorifying the past, Hegel's view tends to absolutism by deifying the state. Liberalism, on the other hand, sought to extend the liberty of individuals and initiated reforms to provide them with external oppor-

[14] For the sake of brevity, the anticipations both of moral autonomy and of individual liberties by earlier thinkers like Locke have been omitted.

tunities. Its weakness from the beginning has been its atomistic psychology and its hedonistic morality, both of which have tended towards externalism. Marxism turned its back upon the Liberal doctrine of individual liberty. In effect, man becomes an economic animal, loses his identity in a social class, and relinquishes his political and intellectual freedom to the state in return for economic security. The vitalistic conception of man developed by Nietzsche and other naturalists reduces the will to vital force and its freedom to power over others. Meanwhile individualistic democracies based upon the earlier Liberalism are giving way in many countries to collectivistic tyrannies based upon economic determinism or nationalistic lust for power.

The conclusion seems clear: one-sided conceptions of freedom, resting upon inadequate conceptions of the self, always lead either to the paralysis or to the destruction of complete freedom. For example, if the root of moral freedom in the will is lost sight of, personal initiative is sacrificed to external opportunity. If, on the other hand, the moral freedom of the will cannot find or create social institutions to aid it in fulfilling itself, it is rendered ineffective. The only way to avoid these and other dangers to freedom is to conceive it in relation to a concrete and adequate view of personality. If we allow ourselves to fall into abstractions, as writers do who identify man with reason, or good will, or economic acquisitiveness, or will to power, our understanding of freedom becomes confused. Man in the concrete is more than rational man, or economic man, or political man, or struggling animal. Man is a mixed creature struggling to elevate his whole life to the level of spirit, as we argued in the last chapter. Hence, all of the needs of his complex self must be met, and met in a way which will be consistent with his spiritual destiny. Now, this involves the recognition of several modes or levels of freedom, no one of which can be neglected or denied without imperiling individual and social fulfillment. These may be analyzed separately, provided that their interdependence in the self is clearly realized. They are related to one another in definite ways, and they are all to be justified by reference to the goal of spiritual personality. Let us consider briefly each of these modes of freedom, its nature, its limitation, and its contribution to personality organized at the spiritual level.

In the first place, there is *freedom of impulse*. It has to do with the impulses or tendencies which we share with other animals and which serve in the first instance for the maintenance and perpetuation of life. We speak of impulse as free when it arises spontaneously and moves to its fulfillment without obstruction. The natural impulses of human beings seldom if ever move to their fulfillment without the will coming into play to endorse or approve their expression; and they are constantly being obstructed by forces within and without. Nevertheless, men often tend to think of this kind of freedom as the most important freedom they have, because it is fundamental for the continuance of life. Without freedom to fulfill our impulses to eat, drink, sleep, love, and the like, it is obvious that life could not go on or higher interests be developed. Moreover, their fulfillment gives rise to many of the solid pleasures of life. When we are able to satisfy them as we please—at the time and place and in the manner dictated by our taste—they add immensely to the comfort and delight of life. It is clear, therefore, that human beings need considerable freedom of impulse. We no longer believe that there is anything intrinsically degrading in natural impulses or even that they must distract us unduly from higher interests. Their satisfaction may please the senses, stimulate the imagination, and relieve the strain of life. They not only keep the body alive and healthy, they also give some play to the mind. This is especially true of the play impulse and the love impulse.

But the fact that freedom of impulse is in a sense the most fundamental kind of freedom ought not to blind us to the fact that it is narrowly limited by necessity. Impulse usually rises of its own accord, often when it is not welcome. It is relative to and dependent upon objects of the environment for its fulfillment; and at its lowest level it seems not so much to move itself as to be moved by these objects. We often feel, therefore, not so much that we are free with respect to it as that we are driven by it, even enslaved by it. Moreover, though its satisfaction may give much pleasure, its frustration may lead to profound misery. It may have to remain unsatisfied, or be satisfied only after long delay, or be satisfied with unsuitable and unpleasing objects. In addition, we cannot share with each other the objects upon which an impulse depends for its fulfillment unless we raise it to the level of a common interest. Unless we do so, it tends to give rise to competition and conflict. For its satisfaction usually involves the exclusive use of material things which are limited in quantity. Even when there is co-operation rather than competition between two or more persons in the satisfaction of an impulse there may be disagreement as to the object or action which will best satisfy it, as when friends go to the theater or dinner together, but cannot decide upon a place or a play satisfactory to both. Equally important, freedom of impulse may interfere with broader interests we prize more highly. The freedom of the sexual impulse or of the play impulse is constantly being checked by reflection upon the evil consequences of its indulgence upon our social and intellectual interests. Above all, as we shall see, natural impulse requires external opportunity for its satisfaction, and external opportunity is always limited.

This means, of course, that we can seldom do just as we please, that our freedom of impulse must be exercised with responsibility. Once responsibility is introduced, there can no longer be complete freedom of impulse. When we remember our table manners at dinner, or play according to the rules of a game, we cannot speak of natural impulse as such but only of natural impulse modified by a social context. Of course, we are seldom aware of the thousand and one restraints upon impulse, because education has made habits of them. Such habits have become "second nature," we say; but from time to time the rebellion of natural impulse against them reminds us that they belong to our moral nature and that their presence involves a severe limitation of our natural impulses.

Moral freedom is the second mode of freedom. Moral freedom implies freedom of will in the sense of freedom of choice. Choice follows the presentation of two or more alternatives. It is the possibility of choice between acts which makes possible freedom of will as distinguished from freedom of impulse. Natural impulse does not involve choice; it provides the will with material for choice. Thus, will is the faculty of decision.[15] Deliberation, of course, may be of the nature of what Bradley called

---

[15] In using the term "faculty" here and elsewhere, I do not mean to assume the truth of the "faculty psychology" but only to use terms of popular discourse in a field where I can claim none of the special knowledge of the expert.

a rapid "intuitive subsumption" of the particular act under a principle which has been accepted previously, as when one immediately rejects a certain act as not being "in character." But this does not modify its essential nature.

There are those who refuse to admit any clear distinction between desire and will. Sometimes, they say, we may seem to be undecided while the process of deliberation is going on in our minds, but in reality decision merely signalizes the final victory of the strongest desire. Deliberation on this view is simply a slave of the passions, a powerless spectator of the conflict of desires for supremacy. Hobbes called it an "alternate succession of appetites, aversions, hopes and fears," and he pointed out with commendable candor what, on such a view of deliberation, will must be. "In deliberation," he says, "the last appetite, or aversion, immediately adhering to the action, or to the omission thereof, is what we call the will; the act, not the faculty, of willing. . . . Will, therefore, is the last appetite in deliberating."[16] Now, it cannot be too strongly insisted that there can be no freedom of will when will is conceived in this manner. For will is quite different from impulse. Will does not move us to action as the impulse to drink moves an animal towards water when nothing interferes. Will is the self as originating action. Its action is never the result of a

[16] *Leviathan* (Oxford, Clarendon Press, 1909), pp. 46-47.

single impulse only but is always the expression in some measure of the self as a whole. It may, of course, endorse or approve a particular impulse and act accordingly, but when it does it transforms that impulse by making it its own.

Will in this sense is possible because men possess the function of reason. Reason alone enables man to transcend the relation of the animal organism to its immediate environment, for it alone can present alternative actions, criticize and compare ends, whether near or remote, and deliberate concerning means to the end that is judged to be best. The only possible objection to this view would arise from limitation of the functions of reason to inductive generalization and deductive demonstration. For it is clear that evaluation of ends involves judgments of value of an intuitive nature. But if reason includes intuition, as it obviously does, this objection does not arise. It is significant that we do not blame a person for wrong acts done in ignorance. This means that the will must act on the light it has, and cannot be expected to act on light it does not have.

As persons alone possess will, persons alone possess freedom of will, that is, they alone can direct their actions towards ends determined or selected by themselves. Moral freedom is the freedom of a will which acts under universal principles determined by reason. It is important to notice that this condition is fully met only when we determine our obligations after a review of all the relevant considerations that are known. Often we content ourselves with what might be called "limited responsibility." Sidgwick argues that the principle of egoism, which requires that we seek only our own good on the whole, is as rational as the principle of benevolence, which requires that we seek the good of all men. Egoism may be rational in a limited sense, since it requires reflection upon future as well as present good; but it is not completely rational. It is not rational to disregard the highly important fact that our actions and welfare are bound up with the actions and welfare of other persons. Egoism or enlightened self-interest is not a theory of morality, it is a negation of morality. Moral freedom, therefore, belongs only to the will which submits itself to universal principles determined by reason and endorses the fulfillment of impulses and interests only within the limits imposed by such obligation.[17] Thus, when will acts under universal obligations determined by reason we can speak of it as manifesting moral freedom. We shall consider later the limitation of this second mode of freedom. But before doing so we must deal briefly with a third mode of freedom.

[17] I do not, of course, mean that we are always fully conscious of the rational principle upon which we act or that we always make a review of "all the relevant considerations" before we decide. I mean only that our actions must when necessary be brought to the test of rational principle. Our primary *motive* may be love of our fellows, not desire to be rational; but in crucial cases, at least, we must ask ourselves, what is the rational way to love them?

This third mode of freedom may be called *freedom of opportunity*. It includes political freedom, economic freedom, religious freedom, and the like; and it has primary reference to the external conditions of freedom. The will needs external instruments if its freedom is to be effective. Freedom of opportunity derives its meaning from this fact. As we have said, Hegel derides the "subjective" freedom of the moral will stressed by Kant and exalts in its stead the "objective" freedom made available to men by the society in which they live; and liberals like Mill argue for the extension of a number of specific liberties to individuals by society. Let us try to understand this way of thinking and see how far it is justified.

The first thing to notice about freedom of opportunity is that it is not really a mode of freedom but an instrument of freedom. It is all too easy to forget this. Freedom is initiative, whereas an opportunity is something which is provided in order that that initiative may become effective. An opportunity has meaning only in relation to an end for which it is employed; and if there is no end set by impulse or will, its value disappears. Therefore, freedom of opportunity is secondary to freedom of impulse and freedom of moral will. It cannot be understood save by reference to persons who are trying either to satisfy their natural desires or to make effective their moral wills.

The second thing to notice about freedom of opportunity is that it is social in its origin and nature. Individuals or classes may assert *claims* to economic or political freedom, but unless or until these claims are recognized as *rights* by society they cannot give rise to liberties or opportunities guaranteed by society. It is true that claims are made by and on behalf of persons and justified by reference to their needs. That is the element of truth in the theory of natural rights; for though rights are not innate and inalienable in individuals as such, they are necessary for the fulfillment of individuals. But the claim which society is called upon to guarantee and enforce must be defined and limited by it in accordance with its own demands. That was Burke's point against the exponents of natural rights: normally, at least, society cannot be expected to sacrifice its form of existence as evolved in the past in order to satisfy the claims of individuals or groups. Rights are granted only within the limitations imposed by the nature and resources of a given society. Thus, an external opportunity is not freedom but an instrument of freedom; and that instrument can seldom be provided by society in a form and measure pleasing to all.

In the third place, it is enforced by society. Without the force of society behind it, the recognition of a right by society would have no value. For a right can be secured to the members of a society only if society is prepared to use force against those who would nullify it. In many cases, the number of those who have to be restrained is relatively few. And the primary sanction employed to restrain them need not be physical in the strict sense of the term; it may be psychological, as when farmers are persuaded to conserve the soil and protect the rights of posterity by appeals to their patriotism or their pocketbook or both. But it remains true that rights must be enforced by society in some way.

Now, it is precisely these characteristics, necessary to make external opportunity effective, which render it liable to abuse. Since it is an instrument dependent for its value upon the use made of it, it may be exercised by some or most men in the service of private rather than common ends; in other words, it may be used to satisfy selfish interest without regard to moral will. Moreover, since it has to be recognized and guaranteed by society, it may be denied by those who hold the reins of power, nullified by those who are called upon to enforce it, or withdrawn at any time. Worst of all, since it must have force behind it, it may forge chains which will enslave the individual to the will of the state or a dominant class.

It is easy to find examples of these abuses in Western countries. The use of external opportunities for private or special interests is most characteristic of democracies. Political rights, such as the right to vote or the right to hold office, have been prostituted again and again to the selfish ends of individuals or special interests. Designed to enable all the citizens to participate in the making and execution of public policy, the vote has been sold or the office bought by weak or unscrupulous citizens. The dominant classes have used their ballots, as well as their wealth and influence, to control the organs of government for their own interest, making use of the unscrupulous cleverness of professional men as an aid in exploiting the weak.

But if the perversion of external opportunities by selfish or special interests is the characteristic abuse of democracy, the enslavement of individuals to society is the characteristic abuse of authoritarian states. We have stressed the tendency of Marxists to treat all other rights as secondary to economic rights. The skepticism of Marxists concerning the value of religious, political, and intellectual rights, which are so much prized by liberal democracies, is due in part to the selfish use of them in the past by the dominant classes, in part to the fact that they cannot take the place of economic security. That is the core of truth in the Marxist criticism of Liberalism as a doctrine of political liberty resting upon a basis of economic oppression. If that criticism is not met by the liberal democracies, they will give way everywhere to authoritarian states. But, in practice, the doctrine of the primacy of economic rights leads to the control by a minority party and bureaucracy of every aspect of the common life. Or else it provokes a violent reaction in the form of a nationalistic revolution on the part of those who would preserve and strengthen the nation or their own privileges or both.

I have discussed freedom of opportunity, its limitations, and its dangers, in order to show its dependence upon moral freedom for its sane use. The great discovery of the modern world is that the moral freedom stressed by medieval Christians and by moralists like Kant is ineffective without freedom of opportunity. Conservatives like Hegel, Liberals like Mill, and Radicals like Marx have all contributed to the popular understanding of this fact. We could not, even if we would, go back to the earlier view that most men must be content with an inner freedom while the effective freedom of external opportunity is reserved for the few. But the other side of the truth also needs to be strongly emphasized in our day. If moral freedom depends upon freedom of opportunity for its effectiveness, freedom of opportunity depends upon moral freedom for its wise use, direction, and limitation. For if external opportunities are used for the satisfaction of natural desire without regard to the duties imposed by moral will, they are inevitably turned into instruments, not of freedom, but of slavery.

Moral freedom also has its limitations. For one thing, the reason which determines moral obligation may possess only a partial knowledge, limited as it is by economic interests, national prejudices, and popular errors. Its judgments of value, therefore, may be superficial and the duties it prescribes may reflect a narrow imagination. Besides, to know the good is not necessarily to will the good. The universal principles reason prescribes for conduct may have no hold upon the desires, no control over the emotions. The greatest tragedy of the moral life, perhaps, is that we pay lip service to abstract ideals which we violate every day in our actions. As Aristotle saw, the weak-willed man may know the universal rule but not succeed in applying it to his particular case. It is not the strength of his desire as such that overcomes him; it is the lack of connection between principle and desire. There are usually social and psychological causes for this. Bad moral education may have established attitudes and habits difficult to break or even to modify. There may have been an insufficient or unwise discipline of feeling, that is, appreciation of good and aversion to evil may not have been deeply or rightly inculcated. These are the reasons why honest men through all the ages have had to confess with the apostle, "the good that I would I do not: but the evil which I would not, that I do."[18]

[18] Rom. 7:19.

Thus, the limitations of reason and the weak hold of reason upon desire and feeling may combine to weaken the moral will. But even when it is strong, it may be strained and unlovely. People whose virtues come very hard are more likely to be respected for their strength of will than loved for their goodness of heart. When the will is not accompanied by imagination and sensitiveness to others' needs, it may achieve self-mastery but it will seldom show generosity. Strength and mastery of will may be purchased at a very high price. The moral will may throttle rather than transform natural impulse; and spontaneity of feeling may be all but lost. The battle between moral rectitude and natural desire may have to be fought over and over again, wasting the energies of the self in struggle which might be devoted to creative work. So long as the will is divided, its strength is dissipated in inner conflict. That is why virtue sometimes assumes a more forbidding aspect than vice, or comes to be regarded, even by moralists, as a mere means to ends that are good in themselves, a mere instrument of intrinsic values like beauty and love.[19] Virtue, the Greeks felt, must be beautiful if it is to be completely good. A struggling virtue is an unstable virtue. How, then, can it be regarded as perfect?

These are among the reasons why saints have al-

[19] G. E. Moore seems to approach this position in his *Principia Ethica* (Cambridge, Cambridge University Press, 1903), Chaps. v and vii.

ways been felt to be in a sense "above" morality. They are not above moral goodness, but their goodness is rooted in spiritual love as well as in moral law. Their righteousness exceeds the righteousness of the Pharisees; they do not destroy the law, they fulfill the law, that is, they transcend its letter in order to fulfill its spirit. What is the secret of this higher goodness and of the *spiritual freedom* upon which it rests? The answer is a simple one: when the individual is genuinely devoted to the universal, in other words, when he lives habitually at the level of spirit as we have described it in the previous lecture, his attitude towards his duty is profoundly modified. Duty becomes something that is not merely willed but also loved. What might have been a painful task becomes a happy privilege.

This gives us a clue to the essential difference between moral freedom and the *freedom of the spirit*. The moral will is the self moving towards a good that is not yet attained but is capable of being realized by action. Its freedom is an effortful freedom. Will is the initiative of the self, burdened by the limitations of the self. But the spirit is the self opening itself to universal truth and loving universal good. It is self forgetting and rising above self. It is not so much self striving for the universal as self laid hold of by the universal. The spirit's activity is not initiated with painful effort but lured by the appeal of a higher life. Thus, when devotion comes, duty is rendered easier and at the same time raised to the level of love.

Moreover, the anxiety, the inner division of the moral will is relieved. Unity is achieved in the self through the working of a dominant purpose in it; and the strength which comes from singleness of mind is found. That is the freedom which brings peace. It is not the peace of passivity but of harmonious activity. It is not a peace that is wholly undisturbed but a peace that is able to rise above every disturbance. It is a peace that is superior to evil, not in the sense of being above every temptation, but in the sense of possessing weapons against evil more effective than those of the moral will. William James describes the saint as one whose center of energy has become habitually spiritual, and he points out that for such a person ordinary inhibitions and evils seem to fall away.[20] Spinoza says that one who possesses the highest form of intellect may be freed from bondage to the passions. And all of us have known simple people, who, without claiming to be saints or contemplatives, have attained to a surprising measure of detachment from care and suffering. This superiority to evil, whether moral or physical, indicates spiritual resources in the soul which are seldom tapped save in the presence of misfortune and defeat.

Thus spiritual freedom is that which is achieved through devotion to universal truth and good. It

---

[20] *The Varieties of Religious Experience* (New York, Longmans, Green, 1902), Lecture XI.

leads to love of duty and goodness. It puts an end to the inner conflicts of the self. It gives peace. It is not at the mercy of evil.

Most important of all, perhaps, the significance of our acts is enhanced when they are performed from love of universal good. It is not merely a maximum of values which we seek, as Utilitarians think; it is a permanent meaning in and through our values. This is precisely what the spirit makes possible. Since its activity is directed to values that are of absolute worth for those who seek an ideal universal community of love, it makes us aware of the cosmical importance of our acts and purposes. By broadening our perspective, it enables us to transcend the limitations of self-interest and of self-conscious morality.

Finally, spiritual freedom vitalizes and completes the other modes of freedom we have described. For freedom of natural impulse, moral will, and external opportunity become more meaningful when regarded as functions of a person who is spiritually free. Taken separately, each is an abstraction and has serious limitations. But if one can attain to spiritual devotion, his natural impulses, his moral will, and his external opportunities are at once enlisted in the service of ends that transcend himself, and his group. Every aspect of his personality, high and low, inner and outer, is fulfilled. That way lies the service which is perfect freedom.

CHAPTER IV

POLITICS AND THE SPIRIT

WE HAVE ARGUED that the human spirit has a distinctive nature and a distinctive freedom. But our argument is not complete until we have shown that it can manifest its nature and exercise its freedom in the sphere of social and political conflict. Is it possible for political decisions to be governed by moral principles for spiritual ends?

The thesis that politics should be based upon moral principle is so often stated in an extreme or ambiguous form that it will be well at the outset briefly to indicate what it does and does not mean. First, it does not mean that the forms and functions of government can be deduced directly from moral principles without reference to the concrete interests of a given society. Moral principles cannot be a substitute for accurate knowledge of the many human interests, economic, social, and cultural, which are involved in political decisions. Second, it does not mean that moral considerations can or should determine political forms and practices in detail. Moral principles are relevant in the political sphere, primarily for the determination, not of political forms, but of political ends. It is, of course, impossible sharply to separate the ultimate ends of society from the proximate means taken to realize them, since means and ends mutually determine one another. But, broadly speaking, ethics is competent to criticize means only insofar as they clearly affect the ends which are her primary concern. Third, it does not mean that there is in existence a final and complete set of moral principles which are accepted by all and which can be applied to political problems as the laws of physics are applied to engineering problems. Since there is no such authoritative system of ethics, the moral principles that are applicable to political issues are primarily those which are actually held by political leaders and private citizens. It is necessary to add, however, that the moral convictions of citizens and their leaders are constantly undergoing change under the influence of moral philosophers, prophets, and reformers in all walks of life. Fourth and finally, it does not mean that the state is wholly a moral entity. The state is at once natural and potentially moral, natural in its foundation in the common needs of life, moral, at its best, in the ideals of its citizens. The natural aspect of states is what all political realists, the moral ideal what all political idealists, insist upon. Both are

POLITICS AND THE SPIRIT

right in what they assert but wrong in what they deny. For the state arises, in part at least, out of the natural needs of men, but it should be moral and in a sense spiritual in its final intention. In positive terms, politics should be based upon ethics in the sense that the concrete and conflicting interests of the community should be fulfilled only under limitations and for ends determined by the moral principles prevalent among its citizens, in order that the community may satisfy not only its natural needs but also its spiritual aspirations.

With this preliminary statement of what the dependence of politics upon morals does and does not mean, I shall now pass to a consideration of some typical objections to the moral conception of politics. The first of these objections is that which is made by *legalists;* that is, those who attribute undue importance to the existing structure of law or tend to think of the law in abstraction from the broader purposes it serves. In contemporary America the chief danger from legalism in politics comes, not from an open denial of the moral basis of law, but from a confusion of the legal rights of vested interests with moral rights. There is a tendency among conservative lawyers and judges to sanctify the legal rights of property by identifying them with moral rights. This is accompanied by a tendency to deny to the moral rights of underprivileged groups any legal recognition. Nothing could illustrate better the danger of legalism than its tendency to guard jealously the legal rights inherited from the past but to oppose violently all legal rights proposed to meet the changed conditions of the present. Legal rights which have grown up in, and are relative to, a certain social situation are defended as immutable and absolute moral rights. Thus, a moral justification is offered for legal rights which are no longer in accord with the moral convictions of the community as a whole. One of the chief causes for the discredit into which the moral conception of politics has fallen is that it is so often used in this way to protect interests which have little or no moral foundation.

The answer to legalistic conservatism of this kind lies in a clear recognition of the sense in which law is related to morality. Law is, in part, a product of the sense of right which is dominant in a community. But the moral consciousness of a community is not a static thing. The great value of law in preserving continuity with the past and in establishing a system of order must not blind us to this fact. Why are law and order so often regarded as enemies of liberty and progress? The reason is not far to seek. If they are unjust in their incidence upon present-day society, they may strengthen the chains that bind the weak and poor to the strong and prosperous. They may provide a front of legality for evasions of duty and for irresponsible practices which would otherwise be condemned as vicious. Thus, they may lull us into a blind and complacent acceptance of the wrongs and sufferings of large numbers of people. Laws inevitably become static unless they are continuously subjected to the criticism of the moral consciousness of the present as it responds to the needs of the present. Just because law is the guardian of order and justice, it must not be allowed to petrify. It is the ally of reason against impulse, but it must not become the ally of death against life. In short, the legal rights inherited from the past must be brought into conformity with the moral consciousness of the present, and new legal rights which are demanded by changed conditions must not be discountenanced merely because they are new.

The political *realist,* unlike the legalist, openly denies or minimizes the moral basis of politics. In brief, he insists that the basis of the state is self-interest backed by force, and that reason and right are quite subordinate if not powerless factors in it. He sometimes rests his case upon the historical origin of states in force. The answer to this argument is that, even if conquest may have been the origin of every state, its present function includes at least the protection of life and the provision of some of the external conditions of a good life. The strongest argument of the realist, however, is that without force, law would disappear and men would relapse into the anarchic "state of nature" described by Hobbes. Now, this is doubtless true, but it is not the whole truth. Positive law does depend in part upon compulsion for its effectiveness. But it must not be forgotten that it is dependent for its efficacy upon other factors than force. If men are not inclined to obey it, there is seldom enough force to compel them to do so. Experience with the Prohibition Amendment and the speed laws brings home to us the weakness of positive law in the face of widespread nonobservance. Moreover, even if law depended exclusively upon force for its efficacy, it would not follow that it depends upon force for its form and purpose. It is true that law needs force to compel obedience to it; but it is equally true that it needs reason and right to *create* and *justify* it.

Charles Merriam has shown clearly the impossibility of divorcing political power from the ends and purposes served by it.[1] After a descriptive analysis of the ways in which power arises out of group conflicts, he discusses the moral bearings of power. In the first place, power can maintain itself only under definite moral conditions. Those who exercise it must reward and punish correctly, keep order and secure justice, and plan and provide for the common welfare. They must rule in the interests of others or at least convince others that they are doing so. In the second place, they cannot outrage the moral be-

[1] *Political Power* (New York, McGraw-Hill [Whittlesey House], 1934), pp. 215 ff.

POLITICS AND THE SPIRIT

liefs of their followers beyond a certain point. They may challenge the moral beliefs of some if they will appeal instead to the moral beliefs of others. But they cannot live constantly above morality. As Merriam puts it, "no ruler can be continually immoral or typically immoral for this would involve antisocial tendencies incompatible with the exercise of the social trusteeship which he professes."[2] In the third place, the exercise of power depends upon the abnegation of the community. "The powerholder assumes that in the community there is the impulse to surrender and sacrifice.... The ruler is a function, an instrument, a means of the community, not an end in himself.... He may be so intoxicated by his apparent authority that he forgets or despises the gentler impulses upon which all his pride rests in last analysis, but the community does not forget its own basic purposes and doom dogs his footsteps."[3] If, then, power is maintained only when it is believed to be exercised for the community, when it is restrained by the moral standards of the community, and when there is moral submission of the citizens for the sake of a common good, it is not realistic to say that politics is a matter, not of moral ends and purposes, but solely of power.

The political realist might, however, admit this without surrendering his main contention. The possessor of power, he might say, does indeed have

[2] *Ibid.*, p. 216.   [3] *Ibid.*, pp. 232, 233.

to exercise his power in such a way as not to shock the moral convictions of his people nor seem to neglect their good. But a ruler may *seem* to share the moral and social idealism of his people while in reality he is concerned only with the maintenance of his power. Indeed, the most successful rulers are just those who have so completely identified the interests of their own people with their own ambition that they have hardly realized that their real motive was power. In other words, it may be true that the ruler must conform to the moral ideas of his people, but his conformity may be merely instrumental or incidental to his love of power.

To meet this objection we must analyze the nature and function of power in human life. There have always been two opposite views of human power. There is the view expressed by Polus in Plato's *Gorgias,* that men have power when they can do as they think best or as it pleases them to do. On this view, the tyrant is the most powerful man because he has control over the lives and property of other men, to do as he pleases with them. A frank justification of the will to power is offered by Callicles in the same dialogue. Right is simply the rule of "the superior" over the inferior in the interest of the rulers. Callicles means by "the superior," he says, not simply the physically stronger, but the men of intelligence and daring. But though he emphasizes in this manner the superiority of aristocrats rather

POLITICS AND THE SPIRIT

than brutes, his main argument consists in a frank appeal to a "law of nature" according to which the stronger species of animals dominate the weaker. In this argument, insofar as he compares human superiority to biological domination, he abandons ethical evaluation for biological description. But he also states his argument in terms of a hedonistic ethic. The good, he says, is the gratification of desires as frequently and intensely as possible, since in this way the maximum of pleasure is attained. Ordinary temperance and justice impose limits upon gratification and must therefore be regarded as virtues "according to convention" only. They are, therefore, appropriate to the weak but out of place in the strong. He who by virtue of his superiority possesses the power to command his fellows will be able to gratify all his desires and secure the greatest pleasure. Such a man is good "according to nature"; and justice or right, in morals and politics, is what he decrees and enforces by his power.

The other view of power is that expressed by Socrates in his reply to Polus and Callicles. Is it really true, as Polus thinks, that a man possesses power insofar as he is able to do as he pleases? What if doing as he pleases prevents him from attaining his real good? What if that which to natural impulse appears desirable is seen by reason not to be the good he rationally wills? Is Callicles justified in thinking that the satisfaction of all kinds of desires without discrimination or limit is what men want? Must there not at least be a rational principle to discriminate between good and bad pleasures? If so, is that not an indication that we do not want mere satisfaction as such but an ordered and temperate life? May it not be that the tyrant, far from being the most happy man, never gets what he really wants at all but sacrifices the good that could satisfy his will to a round of momentary pleasures? How, then, can a man who never gets what he really wants be said to be either powerful or happy?

Socrates' refutation of Polus and Callicles may strike the hasty reader as sophistical. In effect he seems to say that only a virtuous man can have power and that a tyrant is powerless because he uses his power to please himself. Is power, one asks, possessed only by those who seek moral and rational ends? Is it not a potentiality capable of being turned either to moral or to immoral use? If so, must we not agree with Polus that the tyrant possesses great power, however much we may disapprove his use of it? But this objection, true as far as it goes, completely misses Socrates' point concerning power. He is not denying that a tyrant like Archelaus has the power to imprison, ostracize, or even execute anyone he pleases. His point is that this is the kind of power suitable to a brute rather than a man. His argument concerns power, not as a mere physical or biological force, but as a human function. *Human* power is that which carries out human will for human good. It is the capacity to fulfill purposes distinctive of a man, not to indulge one's appetites and bully one's fellows like a brute.

The bearing of this upon the moral basis of political power is obvious. Callicles had asserted that a ruler will govern to his own advantage, taking more of the good things than he allots to others. But human rulership, Socrates replies, is an art; and, like every art, it consists in realizing a certain purpose in a certain material. As the doctor practices an art which maintains the health and order of the body, the statesman practices an art which maintains the health and order of the souls entrusted to him. This is another way of saying that the function of the ruler is to serve the good of the citizens, and that political power is simply an instrument for carrying out that function. But, it may be objected, this is to define political power, not as it is, but as it ought to be. Socrates would not for a moment have denied this. In the *Gorgias* he shows that he has no illusions about politicians as they are. Even Pericles, he says, did more for the walls and harbors of Athens than for the character of Athenians. His point is that politicians who do not serve the common good are not carrying out their function as politicians, they are not practicing the human art of statecraft at all.

The assumption behind this conception of political power is that it must be defined in normative terms since it exists for the realization of human good. Politics, like morals, is a practical art which rests upon knowledge of human nature and its distinctive good. Now, it is this assumption which exponents of the "politics of power" have always refused to believe. The rulers, they think, must be related to the ruled, not as to persons, but as to things; not as to rational beings who are ends in themselves, but as to dumb animals destined to serve the ends of their masters. They hold a cynical view of human nature which degrades men to the subpersonal level of domesticated animals at the best or caged beasts at the worst. The issue between Callicles and Socrates is therefore the fundamental issue of politics. Is justice the will of the "superior," that is, the stronger? If so, it cannot also be the good of the people. Is power the ability of the "superior" to do as they please? If so, it cannot also be the capacity to fulfill the function of men as distinguished from brutes. Is the ruler one who takes the lion's share for himself? If so, he may be a strong lion but he is not a good ruler. Socrates' conception of the ruler and his power is simply an assertion that men should live together and treat each other, not as brutes, but as men.

The Greek tyrants approved by Callicles differed in certain respects from our contemporary tyrants. They were tyrants of small city-states; their modern imitators are tyrants of great national states. They ruled mainly for personal glory and the satisfaction of appetite; the tyrants of our age rationalize their tyranny as necessary for economic security or national greatness. They were limited to the ostracism or execution of their enemies and the temporary ruin of the city; our modern tyrants control the fortunes, the cultural aspirations, and the very lives of millions of men. Our modern tyrants, therefore, are far more dangerous and destructive than the tyrants Plato knew. With greater force at their disposal and greater numbers under their rule, they exert a deeper influence upon the lives of men. They can transform the lives and values of whole peoples and set great armies marching. They can even pervert the moral strength of men, using their capacity for heroic devotion to enslave them to fear, hate, and war. Under such circumstances, the victory of Socrates over Callicles is not an academic question, it is a question of the life or death of modern civilization.

We have been considering the doctrines of political legalists who divorce law from the moral consciousness in practice if not in theory, and of political realists who divorce power from its moral function. In a scientific age like our own, however, the subtlest attacks upon the moral conception of politics come from political *empiricists*. Their argument takes the form of a defense of politics as a descriptive science which is neutral on all moral issues. The science of politics, they say, must restrict itself to the facts about the state as it has been and is. We must establish political facts before we venture to set up political ideals or prescribe political programs. Or, as it is more often expressed, we must limit ourselves to the facts and leave it to others to construct ideals and programs. If the question is raised as to whence our ideals and programs are to come, the answer is not very clear. Sometimes the task of constructing them is turned over to moralists, sometimes to political philosophers, and sometimes to practical politicians. It may even be denied that there is any problem concerning them. Why not simply accept norms derived from past tradition or from the consensus of contemporary opinion? At all events, the science of politics can have nothing to do with the discussion of norms if it is to keep its respectability as a science.

Now, political empiricism of this sort is justified, if regarded as an important part of a more comprehensive study of politics. By most political scientists, I presume, it is so regarded. Political science must be descriptive, if political theory is to have a sound basis. There is room within the field of politics for both the specialized political scientist and the political philosopher. Often, though not always, one person combines the two functions; all that is necessary is that he should have mastered his science before he begins seriously to philosophize. With political empiricism in this sense I am in complete sympathy. But when scientific description is taken as the sum and substance of politics as a whole, it divorces the analysis of facts from every attempt to pass judgment upon them. The danger of this is that political empiricism, after giving up moral judgments upon the facts, will turn the facts themselves into moral judgments. "If it is a blunder," Hocking says, "to take what ought to be for what is, it is no less a blunder to take what is for what ought to be.... To say that will, or force, or fact is primary and needs no justification is to say that it is something we ought to accept and conform ourselves to; the fact becomes our standard."[4] The political empiricist, of course, may claim not to be interested in what we "ought to accept" as right, but only in what we must accept as true. But in practice he can hardly avoid deducing standards from the facts he recognizes. Is not the whole point of his doctrine that political norms must be suggested by, or at least not contradict, the political facts? Does this not tend to make facts prior to and determinative of norms?

The political empiricist may, of course, evade the responsibility for evaluating the facts by restricting

[4] W. E. Hocking, *Man and the State* (New Haven, Yale University Press, 1926), p. 74. As we have seen, political realism makes this mistake of taking what (all too often) *is,* i.e., brute force, for what *ought* to be. However much it may try to limit itself to "facts," it cannot dispense with the "ought"; hence, it tends to turn the "fact" into a "norm."

himself rigidly to the point of view of the pure scientist, the role of a spectator of events. For the pure spectator evaluation is irrelevant, for he is not concerned with action. But is such a point of view psychologically possible or even advisable in politics? Surely, to give up political judgment and practice in order to achieve a pure political science would be self-defeating. It is well known that practical experience is an invaluable aid to political insight; yet it would have to be renounced completely by one who wished to be a pure scientific spectator. Are our political empiricists willing to pay that price, in effect renouncing their citizenship for their science? If they are, should their fellow-citizens without protest allow them to do so? May we not insist, with Socrates, that political scientists are the persons who should know best how to practice the political art? I suggest then that the descriptive science of politics is an exceedingly important part, but only a part, of politics; that no one should be more competent, and therefore more responsible, for the further task of evaluating political facts than the political scientist; that he can evade this responsibility only by completely renouncing action for the role of the pure spectator; but that, being unable or unwilling to achieve such Olympian detachment from everything that concerns him as a citizen, he is likely to raise the facts of his descriptive science to the dignity of norms, confusing fact with ideal no less thoroughly than the idealist confuses ideal with fact.

Moreover, what would be the content of a purely empirical political science? It may be suggested that political science should restrict itself to an objective analysis of the forms of control exercised by the wills of individuals or groups. On this view, it would describe the methods by which such control is actually effected, without passing any judgment upon the ends for which these methods are employed. Now, I would not question the value of a science of methods, though I am skeptical about the possibility of dealing with methods in complete abstraction from their ends. The question I would raise is whether this is all we should expect from political science. To my mind, society needs help from the political scientist, not only in the analysis of facts, but in the clarification of public policy. At any given time, we may know in a general way what we want, but we do not know how to state what we want in political terms. We need wise guidance if we are to translate our half-formed social purposes and ideals into definite political policies. Of course, we need expert knowledge of methods, but we also need the practical imagination which can bring methods into the service of our ends and purposes. What political forms are most consonant with the form of our life as a whole, past and present? What political methods are most appropriate to our new social purposes? We do not expect the political scientist to determine our values and ideals for us; but we do expect him, together with the practical politician, to help us to formulate our values and ideals in political programs and forms.

It is not the theoretical defenders of political legalism, realism and empiricism, with whom we have chiefly to contend. It is those who are inclined to accept a moral basis for politics in theory but reject it in practice. The rationality necessary for moral practice, they fear, is not to be found in the many, nor can it always be expected in the few. And, supposing men to be far more rational than they actually are, the hard facts of the economic struggle for existence and the political struggle for power make it highly improbable that they will commonly act in a manner consistent with their moral ideals. It will be well to consider this crucial difficulty in relation to democracy, which rests upon faith in the moral dignity of men and in their capacity as rational beings to determine their common good for themselves.

The charge that men are not rational in their political decisions usually means that they are short-sighted or selfish or both. Some of those who level the charge emphasize the impulsive and passionate aspect of men's conduct, others the poverty of their imagination and the consequent provincialism of their thinking, and others their inability to deal with the complexities of political life. There is much truth in the charge in each of these forms; and the defenders of human rationality should admit it without question. But in addition to the fact that the low average of rationality is to some extent due to limited opportunity, I would point out that the time factor must not be forgotten in estimating political rationality. A person's political judgment is not necessarily determined by his vote in a given election—few of us are proud of all of our votes as we view them in retrospect—but by his capacity for changing his political opinions under the pressure of facts.

The logic of facts has great potency in political thinking. A major depression may radically revise a person's political opinions or serve to accelerate a revision already begun. Such large-scale facts as unemployment, the Negro problem, and farm tenancy are the most insistent, the most unavoidable of facts. And the newspapers and political parties apprise us of issues that would otherwise escape our attention. It is, of course, true that the tardy correction of errors in political judgment is often a costly process; indeed, false opinions may be fatal where time is of the essence of the matter. But that is the general tragedy of our human lot as finite and fallible beings, and democracy offers through free discussion and regular elections at least as good a chance for the correction of major errors as other forms of government. Moreover, it must be borne in mind that major political decisions are made on issues that are broad and fundamental, since they concern the basic conditions of life for many citizens. For this reason, it is easier for common people to grasp them than it would be if they concerned the more subtle issues of the intellectual and spiritual life. Indeed, it may be argued that common people are more likely to think sanely on broad social issues than are intellectuals and aristocrats. Their lives are often touched more vitally by such issues than are the lives of those who can shield themselves in a measure from the impact of harsh realities. And they are, as a rule, not less socially minded or morally responsible than the rich and proud who feel superior to them.

However, I would not be thought to take for granted the rationality of men in the political sphere. Men are only potentially rational, and it is by hard and costly experience that they develop their rationality. It is unrealistic to exalt the good sense of common people as such; indeed, one of the most dangerous tendencies of modern democracies is to treat *vox populi* as if it were *vox dei*. The truth is, intelligent and courageous leadership is needed under democracy at least as much as under other forms of government, for the people must be helped to exercise wisely their responsibility in the framing of public policy. The argument for democracy is not that the people are wise enough to govern themselves without leaders but that it gives an opportunity for the development of leadership wherever it shows itself. A critical democratic theory does not glorify the people as such, it puts trust in the people only when they develop, choose, and respect capable leaders. The potential rationality of the people can be developed only through rational leadership. It must be remembered also that the people make their political decisions, not by their own limited intelligence alone, but with the help of a cultural and political tradition which they have inherited from the past. This tradition includes, not only a constitution, but also a mass of political treatises, biographies, and laws. It serves to school the people in principles and ideals which they can take as premises for their political thinking. As rational ethics presupposes customary morality, political rationality presupposes political habits and traditions. Thus, we cannot assume the rationality of men as a given fact. But we can believe in a certain development of potential rationality with the aid of wise leaders and sound traditions.

The most formidable criticism of men's rationality, however, we have yet to face. Men are not only limited in intelligence, it is often said, but they are also incapable of rising above their individual, class, or national interests. Under favorable conditions such as those which prevailed in Western democracies during the last century, the warping of judgment by interest may not be fatal to democracy. So long as economic expansion continues and the political parties are in substantial agreement, no serious conflict of interests need arise. But under less favorable conditions, there may develop such a sharp divergence of interests between powerful classes that compromise is impossible. In such cases, democracy is all but doomed. This is the thesis which was recently developed in such a persuasive fashion by Professor Harold Laski.[5]

The argument has a peculiar fascination in our day as we watch bitter conflicts between classes, nations, and ideologies develop to the point of open warfare. The dynamic of discontent in dissatisfied classes and nations at times seems to be driving us irresistibly towards disaster. At such a time it is difficult to retain one's faith in the human spirit and its rationality. The issue is a difficult one, and I am not competent to deal with the political and economic aspects of it. I do wish, however, to comment on the assumption which seems to lie behind the argument. It is the double assumption that man is primarily a creature driven by natural desires which must be satisfied by material objects and that reason is little more than a means to ends determined by such natural desires rather than by reason itself.

[5] *Democracy in Crisis* (Chapel Hill, University of North Carolina Press, 1933).

Once this assumption is made, it of course follows that reason must be controlled by economic interest and that basic conflicts of interest will not be submitted to the bar of reason. It is an assumption to which we have become accustomed under the influence both of classical and of Marxist economics. Moreover, it reflects the dominant attitudes developed by unrestricted capitalism and nationalism. In other words, it is in accord with some of the most powerful intellectual, political, and economic realities of the modern age. That, of course, is why it seems so plausible.

Now it is true that men have natural desires whose satisfaction depends upon material objects. It is also true that the function of reason in relation to these desires is to find material means for their satisfaction. Some men, moreover, live mainly for the satisfaction of their natural desires and use their reason mainly for that purpose. Hence, reason is motivated by economic interest in all men some of the time and in some men almost all of the time. It is well, therefore, to realize that reason may easily become submerged as a result of the conflict of social interests. But it is quite false to say that all the ends of life are determined by natural desires and that reason is only their slave. Even natural impulses are not wholly irrational at the human level, as we argued in the preceding chapter, for they are in a measure transformed when they are taken up into the will. Their objects, their modes of expression, and their meanings are profoundly modified when they enter into relation with social and spiritual interests. For that reason, conflicts over material objects necessary for the satisfaction of desire are not irreconcilable. If desires had to be satisfied immediately by particular objects and if the competition for the possession of these objects were as blind as the struggle of animals for a piece of flesh, economic conflicts would have to be decided by force rather than reason. But satisfaction may be delayed or provided by other objects; and competition may give way in large measure to co-operation in producing and distributing the necessary objects.

Reason, then, is not a slave to desire and interest. It is within men's power to live either as slaves to their private and class interests or as responsible men devoted to the common good. If they choose the former course, they will form personal habits and economic and cultural institutions which will sooner or later submerge their rationality and their freedom. In this way, a civilization or the dominant class of a civilization may all but destroy its higher life. This may lead to the petrifaction of culture and institutions for centuries, as was the case in Oriental countries. In dynamic countries of the West, it is more likely to lead to the revolutionary overthrow of the dominant class by a more vigorous one or even the widespread destruction of civilization by wars. In short, when men refuse to follow reason, they pay a terrible price of disintegration, tyranny, and death.

It may serve to give point to our defense of the moral conception of politics, if we inquire into the moral basis and spiritual ideal of democracy. For this purpose, we must distinguish carefully between democracy as a process and democracy as an ideal. Though it is with the latter that we are chiefly concerned, the importance of democracy as a process must not be overlooked. For the techniques which have been developed by democracy are essential to the participation of the people in the formulation of public policy. Without free discussion, for example, important interests and opinions of the citizens are sure to be neglected. Without regular elections, this discussion would be academic and pointless since no decision could be taken. Without universal suffrage, the decision taken would not represent in any sense the whole community. Without majority vote, the dominant will of the community could not be determined and the conflict of group interests would render united action impossible. Without representative government, the dominant will of the majority could not lead to the formulation and execution of laws and the minority could not make its criticisms heard through an official opposition. In short, democracy cannot be a reality, where there is not free and continuous discussion of public issues leading to decisions by majority vote at periodic elections in which representatives are empowered to give definite and effective expression to the dominant will of the community. The importance of this process is that it makes possible deliberation and decision by members of the community concerning their common purpose.

I am aware that the actual working of the democratic process falls short of the theory behind it. There has been much discussion in recent years of its failures and various proposals have been offered for its improvement. What I am concerned with, however, is the moral presupposition which lies behind the process. It is assumed that there is a community capable of formulating a common purpose and that all the members of the community have a moral right to share in the process of formulating that purpose. Since this presupposition has been vigorously challenged of late, it calls for at least a brief examination. For if it is rejected, all attempts to improve the process based upon it will be doomed to failure from the outset.

In an interesting essay, A. D. Lindsay has defended the concept of a common purpose. "In a society small enough for common discussion," he says, "there does emerge something which can only be described as what the society has willed. . . . The decision of the society is the result of all its members contributing to the discussion. It has come about by the individuals willing and thinking together.... When men who are working together pool their experiences and share their difficulties, there can and often does come out of their decisions a decision which is really the decision of the society, which no individual could have come to of himself, and which each yet recognizes as more completely carrying out the purpose of the society than his own original suggestion."[6] E. F. Carritt criticizes this argument on the ground that out of such a discussion "there can and often does result a compromise which may be approved by nobody and worse than the more consistent proposal of any individual member."[7] Now, this criticism seems to me to miss the point of the argument for a common purpose. It is true that a compromise between the various proposals put forward by different individuals may represent a mere mechanical combination of their conflicting opinions; but it is often possible to synthesize conflicting proposals by finding a principle of unity which reconciles them. Of course this is more likely to occur in a small association such as a church or university than in a large political entity such as the national state. But the possibility of an approximation to it by the state cannot be ruled out a priori. Moreover, Carritt does not realize that what a com-

[6] "Bosanquet's Theory of the General Will" in the *Proceedings of the Aristotelian Society*, Supplementary vol. VIII.
[7] *Morals and Politics* (Oxford, Clarendon, 1935), p. 204.

promise may lose in strict logical consistency it may gain in inclusiveness and practicality. Political proposals are compromised, not primarily with a view to arriving at abstract truths, but with the aim of adjusting conflicting interests and opinions in a way that is practically satisfactory. It is often more essential that the different members of the community be honestly consulted and the different interests of the community carefully considered before the decision is reached than that the decision be perfectly consistent.

But Carritt's objection to the concept of a common will and purpose goes deeper than a mere dislike for compromise. He is afraid that it will lead to an idealization of the state and a subordination of the individual. For this reason he rejects it and bases all political decisions upon the duties of individuals to recognize the rights of other individuals.[8] But surely the ground of my political responsibility or obedience is not simply the rights of individuals as such, but the fact that I ought to do what is best for the community as a whole, to help realize its common purposes. It is true that these common purposes derive their significance from the fact that they fulfill the needs of individuals. They are not the purposes of a mystical entity, the "State" or the "Race," but of the persons of the community. But membership of persons in the community, with its common

[8] *Ibid.*, p. 186.

history and institutions, is a vital factor in their lives. In their political decisions, therefore, they must not merely recognize the rights of other individuals, but also try to give form to the life of the community.

The sense in which we speak of a common purpose of the community may be clarified by pointing out that detailed agreement upon that purpose is not present at the beginning but is achieved by the democratic process of discussion and deliberation. It is possible for persons to desire the same end without agreeing as to the best means to realize it or as to the share each should have in it when realized. They may even differ at the outset in conceptions of the end itself, especially if it is complex. All that is required in a democracy is that each should be loyal to the common end and co-operate with the others in the effort to realize it. Their initial disagreement as to the content of the end, the proper means of realizing it, and their relative shares in it is not final; it simply raises a problem that may be solved by discussion in a spirit of conciliation. Of course, the problem of attaining agreement as to the common end or purpose of a great nation like ours is a very difficult one. For the end is a complex of many elements and their relations, and the means are both complex and uncertain. But if mutual respect and willingness to compromise are preserved, the problem can be progressively solved by the democratic process we have described.

It is sometimes objected that a "common" good or purpose by its very nature cannot also be "my" good or purpose. There are some conceptions of the common good whose abstractness lays them open to this objection. But if the common good is conceived concretely as including the individual good of the persons of the community, as it is in a democracy, this objection disappears. As Joseph points out, the community may set up a "common good" or "form of life" without sacrificing "my" good or "your" good to it.[9] For a common good is not an abstract uniformity but a concrete system in which each desires the good of the others and through sympathy makes it his own. It will be remembered that we argued in the second chapter for a concrete rather than an abstract conception of the universal to which the individual devotes himself. We also pointed out that devotion to the universal conceived in this way as an ideal community of all men is compatible with devotion to the actual communities which mediate the universal to men. This is especially true, I should hold, when the actual community in which one lives is genuinely democratic. For though it is a mistake to identify the ideal universal community with democracy, it is also a mistake to deny that some forms of government are far more remote from that ideal than democracy.

[9] H. W. B. Joseph, *Some Problems of Ethics* (Oxford, Clarendon Press, 1931), p. 117.

The fact that there is no logical contradiction in the concept of a common good does not meet the major practical question. What is the actual basis upon which the common good of a community rests? What force can be relied upon in a democracy to create a sense of common good? If we are to answer that question, we must break decisively with the view that individualistic attitudes and habits are compatible with the common good of a democracy. It is sometimes assumed that, if crude individualism can be transformed into enlightened self-interest, it will serve as a basis for democracy. It will then not be necessary to appeal to public spirit, for within the framework of external order maintained by government the self-interest of individuals and groups may be asserted without limit. Despite its popularity, this conception is thoroughly false. It is true that a democracy with little inner cohesion between its constituent elements may maintain itself for a time under favorable conditions. As long as no major challenges are offered to it from within or from without, it can hold together as a loose confederation of interest groups, each of which derives advantage from its law and order. But a fundamental issue such as slavery will rend it asunder, a severe and prolonged depression will array its classes against one another, and a major war will threaten its very existence. In short the individualistic conception of democracy is both ignoble and dangerous.

The factor that has been most emphasized in modern democracies as offering the basis for a common good is the sentiment of nationality, produced by a common race, culture, and history. Burke vindicated the importance of bonds of sentiment which have been forged by association through centuries of history. He thought of the development of social sentiment as in large part a process of natural growth like that of an organism. The rational wills of the individual citizens he treated as a secondary factor. As a result, he sometimes seemed to regard the solidarity of the state as a mere matter of habit and feeling, sustained by the momentum of the past. Herein lies his chief mistake. Social sentiments, though deeply rooted in the natural feelings and habits of men, must be sustained also by conscious awareness of their meaning and deliberate devotion to their maintenance. Moreover, the citizen is constantly being called upon to respect the rights of other citizens with whom he feels little natural sympathy or cultural solidarity. This is especially true of a country of such vast size, brief history, and diverse traditions as our own. In modern industrial civilization the weakening of social relations and of the sense of continuity with the past makes it harder than ever before for democracies to rely mainly upon the sentiment of nationality and the sharing of historical tradition. At most, this provides the natural basis of a common purpose; and, combined with the economic advantages derived from the association of individuals with one another, partially explains the obedience of citizens to the laws.

But a third factor, moral responsibility touched by spiritual aspiration, is absolutely necessary if a common good is to be recognized and served with fidelity by a democratic people. The state is maintained, from the outset, not merely by self-interest and social sentiment, but by moral will. In order to guarantee their freedom, men must establish and maintain a system of laws. Their common will for a responsible freedom is the rational basis of the state. Moreover, to the extent that the community inspires their devotion as well as demands their obedience, the moral will of the citizens is strengthened and exalted by spiritual devotion to the higher aspirations of the community.

If the democratic process thus derives its meaning from its relation to the common good of a community united by a moral and spiritual purpose, our modern democracy has obviously fallen far short of its ideal. Western democracies have often extended liberty without requiring moral responsibility in its use. As a result, they have permitted the most appalling economic inequality, and they have almost lost the idea of a spiritual good dominating the common life. That is why there is so much talk of revolution in democracies. Revolutions are the work of those who have been shut out from the economic and spiritual advantages of a community until they have ceased to feel that they share in its common life. The most significant commentary upon the destructive effects of laissez faire individualism on the organic unity of the modern community is the Marxist theory of class warfare. That theory merely reflects a system which has arrayed employer and laborer against each other and has all too often made of democracy itself the instrument of the dominant economic class.

It is obvious, therefore, that democracy must be built more securely upon moral and spiritual foundations if it is to be worthy of the name. After all, modern democracy at its best is the expression of an ideal of man as essentially moral and spiritual. In part, it rests upon an extension to all men of the Greek belief in rationality. For the right of the common man to have a say in his government implies a capacity on his part to exercise that right as a rational being. In part, also, it rests upon the Christian belief in the intrinsic worth of human beings. As persons, men have a dignity and worth of a different order from that we attach to things. They may not be used merely as means to the ends of others; as Kant says, they are ends in themselves. Combining the Greek ideal of rational self-determination with the Christian belief in the worth of persons, Kant argued that men possess individual rights only as morally responsible members of a community. Unfortunately, most nineteenth-century defenders of democracy stressed rights rather than duties, liberty rather than responsibility. As a result, democracy came to be regarded as little more than a set of political devices such as universal suffrage and majority rule. Its true nature as a venture of faith in the moral and spiritual possibilities of men when entrusted with freedom was all but forgotten.

I suggest that democracy can never attain its ideal until men learn to respect the worth of common people. It is difficult, if not impossible, to respect men's rights when one does not respect men as persons. It is difficult for me to see that another's economic security is as important as mine unless I am convinced that, fundamentally, his worth is equal to mine. I will hardly concern myself for his freedom unless I believe that, potentially at least, he is capable of using his freedom with responsibility. And, even if I grant him grudgingly a measure of equality and liberty, I will not willingly live in real community with him, sharing my ends with him and actively aiding him to realize his own, unless I can feel good will towards him. There can be no real freedom or equality without community; and there can be no real community without mutual respect and good will. We have too long been content to bind our democracy together with the cords of economic interest and national sentiment. What we are slowly coming to see is that these may divide as well as unite, and that the only stable basis of community is mutual respect touched by love. Is it possible to respect and serve men without having some measure of good will towards them?

Is it possible, finally, to have good will towards men without faith in men? But if we go as far as this, must we not go one step farther? Must we not assert once more the spiritual nature of man, his son-ship to God in some sense, as the only solid ground for that faith? Is there any way to answer the challenge that democracies are lacking in unity and idealism if we fail to restore the spiritual conception of man and community upon which all that is best in democracy logically rests?

It is, of course, Utopian to expect any state to be ruled by love. The kingdoms (or democracies) of this world are not likely ever to be transformed into the Kingdom of God. But to the extent to which good will is introduced into the community by its public-spirited leaders and citizens, the state will be leavened by it. The achievements of modern humanitarianism bear witness to the effectiveness of practical love as a political force. It is doubtless important not to confuse the function of the state with that of the family or the church in which love is the norm. The state is primarily the organ of common justice and welfare rather than of love, enforcing the external conditions of the good life rather than persuading men to embrace the life of goodness. But there is implicit in every effort to obtain a measure of justice a recognition of the greater harmony that could be realized by good will.[10]

It is not a fatal objection to the ideal of love that in large-scale social relationships it has to overcome powerful collective egoism, such as the egoism of a class or state. What would condemn the principle of love to political impotence would be the discovery, not that it is difficult, but that it is irrelevant. But if love is interpreted, not as a natural feeling, but as a settled disposition of will to further the good of others, there is no assignable limit to its influence upon political life. Certainly democracy, which depends upon the mutual respect and good will of men for the success of its venture of faith, cannot dispense with it. Democracy without fraternity withers and dies, or, worse, it is perverted to narrow and selfish ends; only when it can breathe the air of a genuine mutuality does it flower and bring forth the fruit that is proper to its kind. Without fraternity there is no real community; and real community is the only effective answer both to individualistic anarchy and to collectivistic tyranny.

[10] Reinhold Niebuhr, *An Interpretation of Christian Ethics* (New York, Harper & Brothers, 1935), Chap. IV.

www.ingramcontent.com/pod-product-compliance
Lightning Source LLC
Chambersburg PA
CBHW030114010526
44116CB00005B/239